You Can Reach People Now

you can reach people now

**JAMES E. COGGIN and
BERNARD M. SPOONER**

BROADMAN PRESS / Nashville, Tennessee

© Copyright 1971 · Broadman Press
All rights reserved

4225-23

ISBN: 0-8054-2523-3

Library of Congress Catalog Card Number: 79-178058
Dewey Decimal Classification: 269
Printed in the United States of America
5.A171KSP

**Dedicated to the Members
of
Travis Avenue Baptist Church
who have made a dream
become a reality**

PREFACE

In a time when many churches are suffering marked decline and numerous others are closing their doors, it is a thrill and a blessing to find one that is on the march for Christ. Travis Avenue Baptist Church of Fort Worth, Texas, is realizing great gains in their strategic ministry for Christ.

This forward-looking church, reflecting the dynamic personality of its pastor, Dr. James Coggin, recently evaluated its past, present, and future. Establishing the center pole of its existance as an outreach ministry, this huge inner-city church built a new program around this priority.

In this volume you find the thrilling saga of a church which took the Great Commission seriously and moved out by faith on the divine marching orders. The statistical growth that has been realized during these months is only a part of the story. The new spirit of enthusiasm and victory which has gripped this large church is another vital ingredient in this success story.

Dr. Coggin relates the events which led up to the momentary decision in these chapters. I had the privilege of hearing this recounted in his office, long before it became widely known. I brought back a number of new ideas to my church, and since these have been implemented, we have seen a marked increase in attendance, enrolment, and baptisms.

I commend this book to every church and pastor wishing to give priority to outreach. Read it all, study it thoroughly, pray it through, and then adapt it to your church and community to the glory of God and the salvation of lost multitudes.

Landrum P. Leavell
Pastor's Study
First Baptist Church
Wichita Falls, Texas

CONTENTS

PREFACE

INTRODUCTION

CHAPTER I
DETERMINING PRIORITIES — 17

CHAPTER II
SKILLED SCHEDULING — 31

CHAPTER III
PLANNED VISITATION — 43

CHAPTER IV
ESTABLISHING ATTENDANCE GOALS — 57

CHAPTER V
A BUS MINISTRY — 67

CHAPTER VI
VACATION BIBLE SCHOOL — 93

CHAPTER VII
FULL USE OF REVIVALS — 103

CHAPTER VIII
TRAINING WITH A PURPOSE — 115

CONCLUSION

You Can Reach People Now

INTRODUCTION

We have come to be the leaders of a new church—a different church—yet it is composed of the same people, located in the same area and in the same buildings. How did this come about? That is the story of this book. Its pages reveal some of the longings of the people of the Travis Avenue Baptist Church in Fort Worth, Texas. Also it reveals some of their accomplishments through the Spirit of the Lord.

Travis Avenue Church has a very impressive past history. For years we heard of the dynamic evangelistic program of Travis Avenue. As students in Southwestern Baptist Theological Seminary we were both greatly influenced by it. It had been singled out far and wide as an example of a soul-winning church. It has been known for its evangelism through the years.

For ten years we had worked, prayed, loved and served together. There had been ups and downs but nothing of any particular significance. We were barely "holding our own." Even that was not easy. We are an inner-city church, a metropolitan church, and this kind of church is not breaking many records in any city today.

We deeply desired to do more than we were doing. We earnestly believed God had more for us than to sit tight preserving our status quo. We mean by this that we felt God wanted us to *reach more people* for his kingdom.

God, in his deep concern and divine love, heard our heart's cry. You see, he was far more concerned about it all than we could ever be. God, too, is concerned about numbers because every number represents a precious soul.

He led us to stop and take inventory. What are we doing? we asked. Where are we going? What is our main objective as a church? What do we really want to do? And how can we do it?

This book is a record of the outgrowth of those days. It is not intended to be a scholarly interpretation. It is not intended to be an example for all churches to follow. It is an attempt to record what happened to one church, Travis Avenue Baptist Church, Fort Worth, Texas.

We have been humbled by the fact that people have inquired about the "new program" at Travis. We have been grateful that many church leaders have been able to adopt some of our methods (as we have been able to adopt other church's methods).

If any other church is in any way benefited by what we have done, this in itself is all the reward we seek.

We decided to write down an exhaustive treatment of the happenings of those days—how they came about, how we found help, the recommendations of the study committee, the application of the various findings to our own church.

Every attempt has been made to answer any question that might be raised. The detailed analysis is made so that any other church desiring to do so could easily understand and apply it to their own program. Certainly, however, we could not in any way assume that churches would blindly take the ideas or programs and use them without careful and prayerful consideration and study.

Each church must determine what it can and should accomplish.

Introduction

The facts recorded in this book hopefully will provide an inspiration and challenge. No one knows more than the authors of this book the great contribution of so many here at the Travis Avenue Baptist Church. It has been possible only because of the tremendous contribution of the study committee and other church leaders and members. One thing that is so striking and yet so refreshing in the work at Travis Avenue is to see the tremendous load that one layman after another undertakes in sacrificial service as a department director, a Sunday School teacher, a training leader, or a bus worker.

A word of special appreciation is due the study committee who worked long and hard hours over a period of months to hammer out the pattern of work that our church now uses to accomplish its work. Members of this committee were: D. J. Singletary, Charles Layton, Joe Lenamon, Jack Hutchison, Martin Hedrick, Cecil Palmer, Eddie Doyle, Mrs. Ralph Drury, Mrs. Ed York, Don Long, Tim Hedquist, Merle Basden, Bill Pearson, and the authors. Also, our deepest gratitude to Mrs. Myrtis Miller, the pastor's secretary, who worked long hours on the typing of this manuscript.

The study and recommendations made to the church would have been of little value had not the people of Travis responded in such an overwhelming way to accept the challenge and to accept what adjustments would be necessary. The results of their efforts are listed below as we compare the spring of 1969 to the spring of 1971. These are only the visible results which express the abiding commitment and convictions that our people have undertaken:

Statistical Report

	1969	1970	1971
Baptisms (Oct.–Apr.)	37	90	257
Resident Church Membership (Apr. 30)	3386	3459	3877
Total Church Membership (Apr. 30)	5766	5893	6339

New Church Members (Letter or Statement) (Oct.–Apr)	178	236	318
New Sunday School Members (Oct.–Apr.)	290	437	751
Sunday School Enrolment (Apr. 30)	2959	3070	3534
Sunday School Average Attendance (Jan.–Apr. 30)	1469	1593	1950
Buses (Mar. 1970– Apr. '71)		35	259
Receipts (18 weeks, Jan.–Apr. 30)	$170,074.62	$189,412.07	$197,398.29

May the statistics above and the amplification which follows serve as an inspiration to our people that this is the greatest hour for our churches all across the land. We are thoroughly convinced "people can be reached *now*."

JAMES E. COGGIN
BERNARD M. SPOONER

CHAPTER I
DETERMINING PRIORITIES

In the spring of 1969 the pastor called together the church staff and a group of lay leaders and challenged them to study a number of key churches across the nation—churches which were reaching people. We selected churches, representing four denominations. Committee members were divided into teams of two and sent out. Each of the teams consisted of a layman and a staff member.

Trips were prearranged with the pastor of each church to be visited. Without exception all were most gracious and helpful. In most instances the committee team arrived on the church field Saturday afternoon and had supper with staff representatives from the church. Prior to the meal, committee members were shown through church facilities and were able to ask questions concerning how the facilities were actually used. During the supper period our host graciously answered questions and gave more detailed information.

The Saturday meetings proved to be most helpful as team members were prepared for their observations on Sunday. Team members usually split up on Sunday to observe different facets of the Sunday School. One would observe the younger age groups while another would observe adults or another age group. Careful notes were taken on the schedule and how the teaching program was carried out. During the worship services notes were taken on the types of music used, the order of service, the starting time of the services as well as the type of message, the length of the message, the manner in which the invitation was extended, and the way people were received during the invitation. Effort was made to observe in such a way that a clear description could be presented to the study committee once the team returned home.

Following the morning service the team would have lunch with another member of the staff for further questions and discussion. On Sunday night the entire program was observed, and following the evening services an after-church snack was planned for more questions and discussions. Often team members would remain on the church field through Monday in order to visit with the staff members, to attend staff meetings and perhaps to have an extended interview with the pastor of the church. After the observations had taken place on Saturday and throughout the day on Sunday, Monday proved to be an outstanding time for making conclusions and getting final details.

A questionnaire was used by the visiting team to compile basic facts about the location of the church, church membership, Sunday School attendance and enrolment, the number of Sunday School workers, the size of classes by age groups, the teaching approaches used, class and department organization, outreach organization, the training program, and the educational level of the pastor and staff members. Each team asked if a worker code was used. Questions were asked concerning the visitation program, its schedule, method of assigning prospects, the purpose of visits that were made, the approach used by the visitors, and the place that the visitation played in the outreach ministry.

The youth area was observed. Questions were asked concerning the use of camping, retreats, and athletics. The Sunday night program was studied. Questions were asked concerning the social life of the church for youth and adults. The weekday schedule was considered. How many nights each week was a faithful member expected to be at church?

Questions were asked about the church budget, the amount of the budget, how stewardship was emphasized through the church, and how the budget was actually handled. Was it a unified budget or was the designated approach to budgeting used? What about the preaching ministry? Was it primarily evangelistic? Was there an emphasis on salvation, or was doctrinal preaching used, or both? Was there an emphasis on expository preaching? Team members recorded the schedule of the services on Sunday, the length, the time of the services. They recorded the part that laymen had in the services and the part that the staff and pastor had. The team tried to learn about the church staff. What percentage were paid staff members? How many lay workers were used in the church program? How often did the staff meet and what was the nature of the meetings?

The music program was discussed. How many choirs did the church have and of what age groups? What was the enrolment and the time of the choir rehearsals? What type of music was used? We tried to get a list of songs sung by the choir, the hymnals used, special music programs presented, Christmas and Easter and other special projects of the choirs, such as retreats, tours, clinics, and so forth.

Teams asked about special programs of the church, such as Bible conferences, revivals, or special recreation events. Public relations were discussed including radio and television ministry, advertising, billboards, and direct mail. The history of the church was discussed. What special ministries were provided for senior adults, for weekday child care, the handicapped, the deaf, the mentally retarded, and college students? Were missions sponsored by the church?

What type of church policy was used? What was the place of the deacons, the committees, the pastor? What were the most difficult problems of the church? Were there divisive groups? Did they need space, financial help, or parking? Were there other outstanding problems? What business administration practices were used? What about food services, janitorial services, and maintenance programs of the church?

All of the above observations were made in the general conversations and recorded on a questionnaire after returning to the motel. A compilation was made by the team members—their impressions, the answers to the questions, and their own conclusions as they felt them. This was all to be presented to the larger committee.

Visiting Teams Reported Findings

After all teams returned, a committee meeting was called for the reports to be given. Two or three committee sessions were needed for all reports to be given. The reports usually consisted of a general description of the church, its location, its facilities and the evident opportunities, or lack of opportunities found. The committees gave highlights of their observations as reported on the questionnaire. They gave suggestions as to how certain ideas or certain approaches discovered might be used in our own church program.

All committees made their reports before any discussion was considered. However, as the reports were given, members of the larger committee had adequate opportunity to ask questions for clarification.

Conclusions Drawn from Church Studies

When the larger committee had exhausted all individual reports and when the compilation was made, numerous observations were startlingly apparent. *First and foremost* was that wherever the committee had been they had found a climate of *confidence* and *victory*.

The pastor, staff leaders, and church members felt God was at work in their church and that the future of the church was bright. This spark of enthusiasm was catching. It was evident in the faces and voices of the committee members as they had returned to report.

The second thing observed was *simplicity* in the work of the church. The organizational pattern was not elaborate; it was not hard to understand, nor was it detailed. Churches emphasized the Sunday School and generally considered it to be the church organized for outreach. The classes and departments were generally much larger than are found normally in our Southern Baptist churches. In one church that averaged about four thousand in Sunday School it was observed there were only seventeen directors or teachers who covered the entire span of organization. Very often in Southern Baptist life a church with an enrolment of three thousand in Sunday School has fifty departments with fifty directors. Here were churches twice that size who could communicate firsthand to every group with only seventeen key leaders.

Not only was the organizational set-up simple but the *schedule* of the church program was very often quite simple. This was not true in every case, but in many of the churches which had the strongest emphasis on evangelism, the only meetings which they had were meetings to go visiting and then one additional night was given for prayer meeting, teachers' meeting and choir rehearsal. It was also noted that most churches felt there was no need for publishing the weekly church paper. (Actually with a simple schedule everyone could remember what was expected of him). There was, however, a small promotional sheet on a departmental level which was passed out to the members who came to teachers and officers meeting.

The third observation made was an *emphasis upon results* rather than upon the process of obtaining results. In other words, as will be mentioned further in the chapter on building attendance, the emphasis was upon people who were won to the Lord and people who actually came and joined Sunday School and church as a result of the visitation. Instead of "counting" people out visiting from various departments each week, they "counted" people won to the Lord by those visiting. *Results* were shared, emphasized and recognized.

The fourth observation was the emphasis upon *the authority of God's Word*. Without exception the churches visited were Bible-believing churches. Teachers were enlisted because they had a conviction about the authority and the authenticity of the Bible as being God's Holy Word. If a teacher could not teach with this point of conviction they simply would not be enlisted. It was also evident that the class discussion was carried out under the strong guidance of the teacher, although discussion and class participation was welcomed. There was no question but that the teacher was a person well versed in the Scriptures and was considered to be an authoritative Bible student. Not only was the teacher to know the Scripture but he was expected to be diligently seeking to live it. A teacher was to bear both the message and the mark of the Christian faith. This was emphasized before the teacher agreed to accept the responsibility of teaching a class.

A final observation on the part of all team members was that there was plenty of *free parking*. Some churches had one parking space for each two people in average attendance. People were not expected to circle block after block in their cars before finding a place to park. The parking was readily accessible, not several blocks away.

Applying the Findings to Our Church

Following the team reports and a thorough discussion of the reports, the hard part of our work actually began. We now set out to make what applications we could to Travis Avenue Baptist Church. The first thing we sought to do was to determine what our overall objective would be. It was the conviction of the committee that our major thrust should be *evangelistic outreach*. In determining this we decided that outreach would be given priority in all that we would recommend to the church. We felt that we could not do everything that we had been doing if we gave major priority to evangelistic outreach.

The greatest example of how we had to change some of our thinking is shown in the following illustration. In recent months prior to our study our church had decided to spend approximately $190,000 for constructing a new kitchen and dining room in our sanctuary basement. We really needed a kitchen and dining room, we thought. We had already paid an architect $10,000 to draw up the plans. However, after our overwhelming conclusion that outreach needed priority, we had to recommend to the church that they rescind the action to build a dining room. We just could not do that and, at the same time, acquire much needed parking area. If outreach was to have priority over dining facilities, then we must provide for outreach by making parking spaces available. The kitchen could wait, so the blue prints were simply laid aside to be used later on.

With our conclusion that outreach must have priority, we also recognized that this would require a great deal of give-and-take on the part of our church leaders. Immediately the staff members and lay leaders alike became aware that all of us would have to be willing to have our schedules changed and to have our particular responsibilities recognized in a little different light.

After many hours of earnest prayer, discussion, and evaluation, the unanimous conviction of the study committee was that we must make our own individual desires subservient to our overall goal—outreach.

Study Committee Recommendations

We, as a committee, were definitely of the opinion that on the basis of our study we had to make some changes. If outreach were to have priority, definite adjustments had to be made. How were we to do this? Would a drastic recommendation for change do more damage than good? Would we create strife, division, and hard feelings? Would the entire church feel as we did—a deep conviction about outreach? How could we lead them to feel as we did? We had earnestly sought the leadership of our Lord all the way through the studies. We had felt his guidance individually and as a committee. We were so definite in our conviction that he was leading us. But how would we influence others to feel as we did?

Again much earnest prayer, much soul-searching, many long hours went into the actual wording of the recommendation to go before the entire church. We began to circulate the information that the committee was soon to have some exciting news to report. Be sure not to miss the meetings. Be on the lookout for the dates. Be praying as the committee is preparing to bring its report to the church.

Before long there was a feeling of expectation and excitement throughout the church. The excitement was spread from the pulpit, through the church paper, and by word of mouth.

Finally the time had come when the leadership of the church felt that NOW was the time to present the conclusions and recommendations of the committee—to the entire congregation. This would be an oral as well as a written presentation.

Announcements were made well in advance of the presentation. Young people and adults were to gather in the church sanctuary an hour before the evening worship service on two different Sunday evenings. Each committee member was asked to sit on the platform during the presentation. They would be available to answer questions. Their presence also indicated their affirmative feelings about what was to be recommended. Each item mentioned was individually considered and individually discussed.

The congregation was then asked to take the information, to study each recommendation carefully, to pray earnestly about all of it, and to be present the following week, same time, same place, for further discussion and church vote.

Below is a list of the recommendations in its entirety. The rest of the book is an amplification of these.

TRAVIS AVENUE BAPTIST CHURCH
Fort Worth, Texas
Church Study Committee Recommendation
As Approved July 20, 1969

Preface:

The report and recommendation which follow are the result of a deep conviction on the part of your pastor, staff and committee. Our increasing concern has been at the point of reaching people. We visited numerous churches of various faiths who have great outreach programs. As a result of what we saw and a careful analysis of our own program we came to the conclusions reached in this report. We definitely believe this to be a great step in the right direction.

A basic "philosophy" must be established by any church and then have all other items in the program relate to this "philosophy." Herein we seek to do this for Travis Avenue. Our main concern and basic philosophy must be "Outreach."

With this in mind several attending conclusions are reached:

1. There must be developed a simplicity in programming so that it is easily grasped in order that everything can be related to the main task —"Outreach."

2. It must be decided that we cannot possibly do everything. Therefore a clear-cut decision must be made as to what will be done.

3. To accomplish the basic philosophy there must be a cutting across of organizational boundaries and a new sense of "oneness" in one task. The report will reveal that the leadership in all organizations have had a willingness and enthusiasm in this regard. When the basic philosophy was decided and these attending conclusions recognized the following recommendations seemed to be the natural outgrowth. Everyone of these will be found to be in complete accord and harmony with the idea of outreach. What might appear to be the minimizing of some things is merely the magnifying of "outreach." As each recommendation is presented relate it to the basic philosophy of "outreach."

With this in mind we prayerfully submit the following:

I. Recommendations Concerning the Forward Program of Advance.

We recommend that the Forward Program of Advance, adopted by the church in September of 1967, be amended to include the following modification and additions:

1. That we postpone the construction of the kitchen facility in the Lower Sanctuary.
2. That the following items be given priority with regards to the expenditure of the building fund:

    A. Expanding and modernization of our present kitchen and dining facility. (Approximate cost—$10,000). The greatest percentage of this expenditure will be for equipment which can be used in the Lower Sanctuary.

    B. The modification of the lower sanctuary so that it can be better used as a fellowship hall until such time as the new kitchen is constructed, (Approximate cost—$2,000).

    C. The acquiring of property in the immediate vicinity of the church and the Property Committee be charged with the responsibility of seeking out new property which the church may wish to buy, and recommending its purchase to the congregation.

    D. The improving of church property to provide additional parking.*

    (* Without exception the churches studied had more than adequate parking facilities to care for those attending as well as future growth. With less than 300 off street parking places this becomes a must for Travis. Because of this need it was deemed wise to postpone the kitchen in the Lower Sanctuary.)

Special Notation:

It is specifically understood that the total cost of the above mentioned items will not exceed the amount of money and pledges in the building fund.

II. Recommendations Concerning the Church Program and Organization

1. Adult

    A. It is recommended that the member training program for adults (Adult Training Union) be planned using the interest group approach as well as the age grouping approach.

    B. It is recommended that units of study be provided, in addition to the regular content areas, to include missions and other subjects appropriate to meet the needs of our church and individual members.

    C. It is recommended that General Meetings for WMS and Baptist Men be eliminated, since mission units of study will be offered during the Training Union hour.

27 Determining Priorities

    2. Youth-in Action (15–17 years of age)
       It is recommended that Youth-in-Action be changed to a special program aimed toward youth outreach and characterized by testimonies, special speakers, musical groups, drama, and informational programs.
    3. Pre-school, Children, and Intermediate Training Program (Birth-14 years of age)
      A. It is recommended that mission auxiliaries and Training Union groups be combined into a unified program of missions and membership training and that these groups meet on Sunday night during the Training Union hour.
      B. It is recommended that training sessions for boys and girls 9–14 years of age be held separately for week to week learning activities but that they be brought together for certain special studies and speakers as desirable.
      C. It is recommended that (a) leaders for the 9–14 year age groups come together for combined planning at such times as provided for by the church and (b) that programs be worked out to insure that all areas of the present Training Union curriculum are included in the total training program of these age groups.
      D. It is recommended that a church wide contest be launched to name the church training program and the age groups.
      E. It is recommended that the G.A. Coronation and R.A. Recognition Service be held on Sunday night during the church training hour.
III. Recommendations concerning Scheduling
    1. Weekly Meetings
      A. Sunday
         9:30 Sunday School
         11:00 Worship Service *
           (* An amendment was made to refer the Sunday morning Sunday School and Worship schedule back to the committee for further study.)
         5:45 Training Union
         Youth Outreach program (Youth in Action)
         7:00 Worship Service
      B. Monday
         7:00 P.M.—Youth Choir (Ages 15–17)

C. Tuesday
   4:30—Selahs
   6:30—The Tabs
   VISITATION OUTREACH (every week)
   Supper and/or report meeting first and third Tuesday
   Special outreach weeks (1st & 3rd)
D. Wednesday **
   5:30–6:15 Food Service
   6:00–6:25 Superintendents and Choir Leadership
   6:30–7:25 Teachers and Officers' Meeting
   Choirs Pre-school
   Intermediate
   Provision for Youth 15–17 (Mission study, Bible study, study hall)
   7:30–8:00 Prayer Service
   7:30–9:00 Sanctuary Choir
   (** Remembering basic philosophy of "outreach" you will quickly see that the entire Wednesday schedule is structured for this purpose. Hence there is no conflict in purpose with the choir rehearsal and Prayer Service being held simultaneously. This served to clear Thursday night and enables faithful workers in the choir to visit on Tuesday.)
E. Friday
   10:00–2:00 Senior Adult Fellowship

2. Monthly Meetings
   A. Class Meetings—Second Tuesday
   B. WMS Groups—Thursday following the fourth Tuesday
   C. Ladies Visitation Luncheon (1st Tuesday).
3. Quarterly Meetings (March, June, September, December)
   A. Committee Meetings, 4:30, 2nd Sunday
   B. Deacons Meeting, 4:30, 3rd Sunday
   C. Business Meeting, 8:00, 4th Sunday
4. Meetings and activities other than the regular scheduled activities listed above.
   A. During special outreach weeks (1st and 3rd Tuesdays)
      (1) No adult activities will be scheduled.***
      (*** The great problem with a visitation program is that a day or time is set and then during the week so many other activities are scheduled that the strength of visitation is

siphoned off. People cannot or will not do two or three things at the church the same week. The action upholds the importance of "outreach" and says it is first.)

(6) Youth and children's activities can be scheduled Friday and Saturday only.

B. During all other weeks.

Adult, Youth, and Children's activities can be scheduled any time except Tuesday and Wednesday.

5. SCHEDULING AND CALENDAR—It is recommended that a definite policy be followed concerning the meeting times of all organizations, that no meeting be scheduled which comes in conflict with meetings already scheduled. Anyone wishing to make a calendar request may do so by contacting the business office. Calendar requests will be coordinated and cleared Tuesday at 9:00 A.M.

IV. Recommendations concerning World Mission Outreach.*

We recommend:

1. That the church establish an annual World Mission Emphasis Week. This would be a church wide effort to involve our total membership in the study of, and prayer for, the overall world mission program of our church and denomination. This week would be in lieu of our present three weeks of emphasis for the various areas of our mission work.

2. That the present three special mission offerings (Lottie Moon, Annie Armstrong, and Mary Hill Davis) be combined into one World Mission Offering. Gifts to this offering would be divided on the following percentage basis:

       70% To Foreign Missions
       20% To Home Missions
       10% To State Missions

(* This will enable the mission program to be more of a church-wide activity. A tremendous impact will be made during the special week.)

V. Recommendations Concerning Worship Services.

That Worship Services be warm, alive, and enjoyable. That each person pray for the Holy Spirit to be in charge and a vital worship experience be a possibility in every service. That the personalities of those involved on the platform be personable and positive. That services not be stereotyped. That each service be planned to include variety, uniqueness, and creativity without being sensational. That special unusual features * be planned every six to eight weeks (probably in the evening services) which would cause greater interest and excitement in the services. That these features be of such magnitude as to attract the attention of the people of Fort Worth and cause the non-church goers to attend the services. This would give added incentive for Travis members to invite friends, neighbors, and business associates to attend the services. It is felt that success in increasing the Sunday evening attendance through these special features would give greater excitement to the lives of church-going Christians and give Travis the increasing image that things are "happening here."

(* We found in a number of churches that this idea constitutes a great means of outreach. We are convinced that it can be most effective and far-reaching here.)

VI. Recommendations concerning Television Ministry

We recommend that the church endeavor to acquire 30 minutes of television time in order to present a weekly outreach oriented program. (This would not currently affect our present television and radio ministry).

Supplemental Notes

1. It is recognized that in light of the above recommendations the Finance Committee may find it necessary to bring specific recommendations to the church concerning the reallocation and modification of our present budget.
2. It is further recognized that additional staff personnel in the youth and adult areas may be needed to fully implement the program of outreach and therefore the Personnel Committee will begin an immediate study to determine our needs.
3. In so far as possible all recommendations will be implemented by Sept. 1.
4. It is also recognized that consideration should be given to the possible establishment of a bus ministry and other outreach activities.
5. The adoption of these recommendations necessitates and authorizes the revision of the Church Constitution.

CHAPTER II
SKILLED SCHEDULING

Sometime back a department director remarked to a member that he had missed him in Sunday School on the previous Sunday. The member replied, "Well, I came to your banquet on Thursday night. I thought that was enough for one week!" Obviously the motivation involved in this instance can be questioned, but the insight it gives into the way many people regard their church relationship is helpful. It seems that Christian people choose what activities they attend. When they are called upon to come for visitation one night, to be in teachers and officers' meeting on another night, to attend choir rehearsal the next night, and then to attend some class or department social function on still another night, there is little doubt that some of these activities turn out to be unsuccessful. The church schedule needs to be planned so that members have time for the priority of evangelistic outreach.

Key Factors in Scheduling

The first factor that we will mention is the number of nights adults are expected to be doing church work each week. As has been mentioned before, in many churches a faithful adult might need to be at church three or four nights each week in addition to Sunday. Obviously there is nothing wrong with people being at the house of the Lord to serve and have fellowship with other Christians. It is wrong, however, for adults to attend these activities and fail to witness to the unsaved and unchurched. When our study committee came to consider the schedule, we discovered that many of our Sunday School department directors were expected to be at visitation on Tuesday, the department planning meetings and prayer meeting on Wednesday, and also at the adult choir rehearsal on Thursday night. If they were faithful to these, little or no time was left for family or personal activities.

After long hours of discussion and with great reservation it was decided that visitation would be set for Tuesday each week and that teachers and officers' meeting would take place on Wednesday night followed by the adult choir at 7:30. This means that adult choir members are not able to attend the prayer meeting service, which also begins at 7:30 P.M. Choir members have their own prayer period during choir rehearsal. This decision was made following the philosophy that Tuesday is a day of outreach and that Wednesday is a day of preparation for Sunday. Sunday School teachers and officers meet for their preparation meetings, then the adult choir meets for its preparation meeting on the same night. All enter into a period of prayer whether in prayer meeting or in adult choir rehearsal. Our most faithful workers are now expected to be present only two nights each week.

Some on the study committee felt that even this would not be enough to focus the time of our members for outreach, so it was decided that the weeks of the first and third Tuesdays would be given over as special outreach week, and that no adult activities would be scheduled during these two weeks. Of course the adult choir and teachers' meetings continue to meet on Wednesday night and the senior adult fellowship meets each Friday from 10 A.M. until 2 P.M. This action meant that by vote of the church no committee meetings, class meetings, missionary group meetings, and no other kind of adult function can be scheduled during these two weeks. This has freed the time of our members so that they can focus in on Tuesday for visitation and on Wednesday for preparation. This idea has revolutionized the outreach program at Travis Avenue Baptist Church.

Controlling Activities

Many people ask, "How do you manage to keep activities from being scheduled during these special weeks?" First of all, the church voted that this would be the plan. It also voted that all activities are to be coordinated and cleared on the church calendar each Monday. Sunday School department directors and other leaders throughout the church are asked to turn in calendar requests listing the time and date desired for activities. This is done with the understanding that no activities are to be scheduled during the special outreach weeks. It is also understood that activities will not be scheduled on Tuesdays of any week. In order to help interpret the program, an annual church calendar is published and mailed into the home of all church families in the late summer. New members receive copies of the church calendar immediately following the service in which they join. A member can look at a given month in the church calendar and see that the weeks of the first and third Tuesdays are shaded, as you can on the sample calendar page. When making their requests for scheduling of activities, they can readily recognize that activities need to be scheduled during other weeks of the month.

Some have asked, "How do you get the people to cooperate?" The answer is that the people were the ones who worked out the plan and they did so with the recognition that this would be necessary if we

1971 FEBRUARY 1971

SUN	MON	TUE	WED	THU	FRI	SAT
JANUARY 1971 S M T W T F S 　　　　　1 2 3 4 5 6 7 8 9 10 11 12 13 14 15 16 17 18 19 20 21 22 23 24/31 25 26 27 28 29 30	**1** Youth Choir	**2** Visitation Ladies Vist. Luncheon Visitation Supper TABS	**3** Correlated Prog.	**4**	**5** Sr. Adult Fellowship Mothers' Day Out	**6**
7 Demonstration Day S. S. Stewardship Assemblies	**8** Assoc. Training Banquet Youth Choir	**9** Visitation TABS Class Meetings	**10** Correlated Prog.	**11**	**12** Sr. Adult Fellowship Sr. Hi Banquet Mothers' Day Out	**13**
14 Pledge Day Singing Churchmen S. S. Stewardship Assemblies Int. Fellowship	**15** Youth Choir WASHINGTON'S BIRTHDAY	**16** Visitation TABS Visitation Supper	**17** Correlated Prog.	**18**	**19** Sr. Adult Fellowship Student-Career Retreat Mothers' Day Out	**20**
21 Training Groups Fellowships	**22** Youth Choir Edna Harr. Soc. Night W.M.S.	**23** Visitation TABS	**24** Correlated Prog.	**25** Day W.M.S. Groups	**26** Sr. Adult Fellowship Deacons Banquet Mothers' Day Out	**27**
28 Victory Sunday Training Planning Quarterly Program Planning	MARCH 1971 S M T W T F S 　1 2 3 4 5 6 7 8 9 10 11 12 13 14 15 16 17 18 19 20 21 22 23 24 25 26 27 28 29 30 31	*Memos:*				

are to major on the priorities we have set for our church. Seldom has it been necessary to go into much detail to explain why a person cannot schedule an activity during one of the special outreach weeks. Very often this is taken care of in department planning meetings or in committee meetings as one member reminds the group that activities can be scheduled only in the other weeks. Also as a leader schedules an activity he can rest assured that when it is placed on the church calendar, his activity will be protected. No conflicting meeting can be scheduled during a time already reserved for others.

The question immediately arises concerning youth and children's activities. The church approved a recommendation which stated that children and youth activities may be scheduled on Friday and Saturdays only during special outreach weeks. This recognizes the fact that our youth and children's age groups need to have activities perhaps when adults could do without them. Children and youth activities other than choir rehearsals are not scheduled Monday through Thursday of these two weeks.

Committees, Deacons and Church Business Meetings

A further step was taken to conserve time and to eliminate unnecessary meetings. Committee meetings, deacons' meetings and business meetings were changed from monthly to quarterly meetings. This means that each meeting is scheduled only one time each quarter. This does not mean that committees, deacons', or church business meetings cannot be held more often. Certain committees need to meet almost every month while others have very little business even at their quarterly meeting. Special deacons' meetings and church business meetings have been called from time to time during the past two years when necessary. Restricting the number of meetings has been a great relief to our church members and the pace of our program has been made more realistic. It does, however, require better planning on the part of committee chairmen and church staff members. During budget planning time the finance committee has scheduled Saturday planning sessions on weeks other than special outreach weeks. These often last for a half day or all day. The church nominating committee starts earlier in the year to do their work, and have also experienced little difficulty.

Timing of General Church Emphases

One of the greatest problems many churches face is that of having too many general church activities, one falling immediately after another. Activities need to be scheduled in such a way that church leaders can effectively promote them and carry them out. When activities are scheduled too close together, one may, in effect, be deemphasized because another had to have the major emphasis at the time.

In many churches, as one enters the Sunday School or a worship service on a given Sunday, he is often met by a new emphasis every week. Each denominational agency, many civic groups and others expect the church to herald their cause. This is done throughout the year until members and prospects enter and leave and never quite comprehend any priority of purpose the church may have.

So in our scheduling it was decided that serious consideration would be given to communicating our priority through what was said from the pulpit by way of message, announcements and all. Otherwise all activities are equated and priorities are not misunderstood. In summary it seems that we communicate our purposes by what we say and do when our people are present. A local church must decide what its focus is and how it will carry this out. Too many activities seem to hinder the ability of a church to communicate its priorities.

Schedule Priority Activities First

One of the best ways to accomplish timing and to set priorities is for church leaders to determine first what the major activities for the year will be. For instance, major activities in a given church might be: September, preparation for the new Sunday School and church year; November, the fall revival; December, Christmas music; February, stewardship campaign; April, spring revival; and June, Vacation Bible School. If these activities are considered to be the major activities for the year, then all other activities need to be planned in conjunction with and in support of them. After the major activities are set up on the church calendar, all other activities have to fit into this pattern or they should be eliminated. It might be necessary for some activity to be carried out only every other year rather than every year. To some extent it may be necessary for a church calendar to be thought of as a continuing series of months rather than in twelve-month cycles. Certain training activities for some groups can be scheduled every eighteen months rather than every twelve. Other activities can be set up every twenty-four months rather than every twelve. Some special events may be scheduled even less often. A church cannot do everything that everyone feels it should do. It must decide what its own program will be in light of its objections or priorities.

Space Emphases for Best Results

Provide enough preparation and follow-up time for each activity. This is necessary if the activity is going to be successful. Consider what the people are doing during the weeks leading up to a given activity. For instance, during the month of December it is difficult to plan activities for the month of January. This is primarily because people are focusing their attention upon the Christmas season. Many business, school, civic, and other community groups plan a special emphasis at Christmas time. Usually in church life special Christmas music or dramatic productions are planned during this time. This makes it extremely difficult to carry out activities successfully early in the month of January. Leaders need to consider this carefully while planning.

During the month of September or the month prior to Sunday School promotion, it is wise to allow time for Sunday School and other program leaders to get ready for the new church year. Many churches schedule revivals or other activities during this month, giving little or no thought to what the people are actually doing. Sunday School preparation week also needs to be planned wisely if it is during the month preceding Sunday School promotion. Very often in our church, department directors and others have pleaded that we not schedule Preparation Week the week just prior to promotion Sunday. Since they are asked to visit all department and class members before promotion day, they needed to spend most of their time during the preceding weeks to get this done. This is not to suggest that preparation week should not be held. It is simply to say that it is wise to plan it in such a way to give leaders time for doing what they have already been asked to do.

It is also wise to consider what the church staff is doing. It is difficult for them to carry out two major activities at the same time and to do them well. Every effort needs to be made to insure that church leaders, as well as staff leaders, can lead in their work in such a way as to do it successfully. One failure because of poor scheduling can set back an entire year's church program or can destroy the future effectiveness of some church leaders. The following pattern has proven helpful at Travis Avenue:

September—Preparation for program organizations
November—Revival
December—Mission emphasis and special Christmas music programs
February—Stewardship emphasis
April—Revival
June—Vacation Bible School
July—Youth activities, such as summer camp or choir tours.

Certainly there will be activities other than the ones mentioned above, but those listed are given the priority of time. For instance, during September workers are asked to visit all Sunday School members in preparation for the fall. Outreach weeks are especially valuable for this special visitation. The second week of the month is sometimes used for a Sunday School training emphasis. The last week is free of any special emphasis so that program leaders can finalize plans for the first Sunday of the new year. The month of October is used for settling into the new year. One Sunday is used for adult class officers' clinic. The month of November is spent largely in final preparation for revival, the revival itself, and for follow-up from the revival. December is filled with missions emphasis and special music presentations around the Christmas Season. The month of January is a checkup month, getting attendance back up following the Christmas holidays, checking the organizations, but no major emphasis is planned. The month of February is given over to a Stewardship emphasis. In March no particular emphasis is planned other than a Sunday School mid-year checkup which takes place during regularly scheduled times.

The month of April is given over to revival preparation, revival services and revival follow-up. Nothing special is planned for May, and June is given over to Vacation Bible School. July and August are used for Vacation Bible School follow-up, but perhaps with a major emphasis going to camps, choir tours, and other youth events.

Obviously every church must decide its own course with regard to planning, but it seems from experience that a major activity every other month is a fair "rule of thumb" approach to church scheduling in our church.

Planning the Annual Calendar

As has been mentioned, we have found it wise to publish an annual church calendar. All program leaders and staff members are asked to turn in calendar requests for the entire church year during the month of May. After the major activities are placed on the calendar these dates are then worked in as near to the dates requested as possible. All dates, however, must subscribe to the plan for special outreach weeks.

As has also been mentioned, each week additional activities are placed on the church calendar as staff members and other leaders make their requests. This is done at the weekly church staff meeting on Mondays. Any conflicts of time or facilities are worked out in this meeting. This may take only five minutes to clear out some weeks, while at other times as much as thirty minutes or more may be required.

In order to clear the weeks of the first and third Tuesdays for outreach, in December it was necessary to set up one night for adult Christmas banquets and another night for children's and youth Christmas parties. Children's and youth parties are scheduled for all departments on the Friday night following the second Tuesday in December.

It will also be noted on the monthly calendar illustration that adult class meetings are scheduled on the second Tuesday of each month.

Class meetings at Travis are considered class outreach meetings. Department and class leaders are urged to invite prospects to these meetings. Teachers and outreach leaders are encouraged to streamline class business and to make this a class fellowship time with members bringing prospects and chronic absentees. Meetings are concluded with a brief devotional thought.

Recap of Schedule of Basic Activities

The following is a recap of our basic activities before and after the new schedule was set up.

	Old	*New*
Committee Meetings	Monthly on first Wednesday at 8:15 P.M.	Quarterly on 2nd Sunday of September, December, March and June at 4:30 P.M.
Deacons' Meetings	Monthly on 2nd Wednesday at 8:15 P.M.	Quarterly on 3rd Sunday of September December, March and June at 4:30 P.M.
Business Meetings	Monthly on 3rd Wednesday, at 8:15 P.M.	Quarterly on 4th Sunday of September, December, March and June at 8:00 P.M. following worship service
Sunday School Officers and Teachers' Meetings	Weekly on Wednesday from 6:30 to 7:25 P.M.	No change
Sunbeams, G.A.'s and R.A.'s	Weekly on Wednesday—some at 5:30 P.M. and others at 6:30 P.M.	Weekly on Sunday at 5:45 P.M.
Choirs: Preschool through 9th Grade	Weekly on Wednesday—some at	Weekly on Wednesday—all at 6:30 P.M.

	Old	*New*
	5:30 P.M. and others at 6:30 P.M.	
Choir: Youth 10th—12th grade	Weekly on Wednesday at 6:30 P.M.	Weekly on Monday at 6:30 P.M.
Choir: Student-Career	Weekly on Monday at 6:30 P.M.	Weekly on Tuesday at 6:30 P.M.
Prayer Meeting	Weekly on Wednesday at 7:30 P.M.	No change
Adult Choir	Weekly on Thursday at 7:30 P.M.	Weekly on Wednesday at 7:30 P.M.
Sunday School Class Meetings	Monthly on Monday at 7:00 P.M.	Monthly to class "Outreach Meetings on 2nd Tuesday at 7:00 P.M.
W.M.S. Group Meetings	Monthly on 2nd Tuesday at 9:30 A.M.(day) and 7:00 (night)	Monthly on Thursday after 3rd Tuesday at 9:30 A.M. (day) and 7:00 P.M. (night)
W.M.S. Day Society	Monthly on Tuesday at 10:00 A.M.	Weekly combined mission study with Brotherhood on Sunday at 5:45 P.M.
Brotherhood	Monthly on Monday at 6:30 P.M. when called.	Weekly combined with W.M.S. on Sunday at 5:45 P.M.

The complete schedule of activities as approved by the church is shown in the recommendation listed on page 27f.

CHAPTER III
PLANNED VISITATION

A few years ago we had a weekly visitation supper on Thursday night. This had been the plan for a number of years. Each week from fifteen to thirty people would gather at six o'clock for supper and prayer and then would go out to visit. Some could visit only forty-five minutes because they had to return to the church for adult choir rehearsal.

Most members had not committed themselves to visit at all, to say nothing of every week. When they were questioned for suggestions, some recommended a monthly visitation emphasis so in the summer of 1967 the weekly supper was replaced by a monthly supper and visitation emphasis. It was understood, however, that we would continue to have visitation each week on Thursday and Thursday night. We also continued a monthly ladies visitation luncheon, which was attended by approximately fifty ladies.

The results of this change were remarkable. On the first night, which was in June, we had seventy-five or eighty people who came, including many department directors and others who normally had not come out for visitation. With this initial success in June we decided to put up posters and to push for a great visitation crowd in July. It worked. Over two hundred persons attended. In August again approximately two hundred came for visitation. It was obvious that many more were becoming involved in the outreach program. During the other weeks of each month records revealed that visits continued to be reported at about the same rate as they had been with the weekly supper. And yet visits reported during the weeks of the monthly supper were greatly increased.

This visitation approach was continued for two years until our new church program was begun. At that time it was decided that we would set aside two weeks each month for a visitation emphasis, the supper on the first and third Tuesdays of each month. The ladies visitation luncheon was continued on the first Tuesday. It was also decided that no other adult activity would be scheduled during these two weeks except for Sunday School teachers and officers' meeting, adult choir, prayer meeting, and the senior adult fellowship which met each Friday. Youth and childrens' activities could be scheduled only on Friday and Saturday during these two weeks. This meant that adult banquets, fellowships, mission studies, training activities, etc., simply had to be scheduled during the other weeks of the month. This was true even during the month of December when Christmas banquets and parties were numerous.

The results of this plan has again been remarkable. We now often have between 200 and 350 people who come for visitation on each of these two special outreach weeks. These special outreach weeks are sometimes referred to in jest as "holy weeks." Some churches have adopted this idea and refer to these weeks as red and green weeks.

The value of this approach was seen last December, when on the third Tuesday, over two hundred persons came out for visitation. In previous years the month of December was almost a total loss so far as visitation outreach was concerned.

Getting the People Out

Although the basic schedule is the most far reaching factor in getting the people to visit, promotion is still necessary. Articles such as this are used in the church paper often.

300 Expected to Visit Tuesday
Supper 6:00 P.M.

At least 300 persons are expected for visitation on Tuesday. Many will visit throughout the day and a great host of youth and adults will come for supper (35¢) at 6:00 P.M. Child care will be provided at 9:30 A.M. to 1:00 P.M. and from 6:00 P.M. to 9:30 P.M.

See that your class or department is well represented.

Announcements are made in each Sunday School department and a supper and child care reservation card is placed on each record book for all Sunday School classes and departments. This is done on

---

```
                    VISITATION RESERVATIONS
                         FOR TUESDAY


Ladies Visitation Luncheon, 12:00 Noon (35¢) _____ plates

Child Care _____ Birth-8 Years _____ 9-11 Years
(9:30 A.M. - 1:00 p.m.)

- - - - - - - - - - - - - - - - - - - - - - - - - - - - - -

Visitation Supper, 6:00 p.m. (35¢) _____ plates

Child Care _____ Birth-8 years _____ 9-11 Years
(6:00-9:30 P.M.)

Dept./Class _____ Signed _____
```

Sunday preceding our special outreach weeks. The sample card shown is currently being used.

The card brings to the attention of each class or department outreach leader the fact that he needs to make an announcement. He also sees this card as something of a report of his efforts.

From time to time a card is mailed out to all Sunday School workers asking them to have their class or department well represented. Visitation is stressed from the pulpit. From time to time visitation report fellowships are scheduled. These may be scheduled on a general church-wide basis or by Sunday School departments or classes. Some groups meet back at homes for homemade ice cream or other kind of refreshments. Others come back to the church. Occasionally all are asked to come back for a general report meeting at which time persons are called on to give "good" reports. By good reports we mean reports of successful visits where some potential results are likely to take place. There is little value in someone sharing a bad experience of how he could not find the address or how someone talked angrily to him. These meetings are simply a time of fellowship and a time of sharing.

How to Conduct Visitation Supper

It should be recognized that the meal served for visitation is intended to be a promotional event. Good quality food is served for thirty-five cents a plate. This is a reduced price from our regular Wednesday night meal because it again gives priority to outreach. An effort is made to make the dining room pleasant by simple decorations. The meal is served quickly so that the time is not wasted by people standing in line.

The meal is scheduled to suit the needs of our people at 6:00 P.M. and every effort is made to dismiss the group by 6:40 so that valuable visitation time is not wasted.

We work to build spirit and proper motivation. Usually a brief promotion meeting is held, using about ten minutes of time. The pastor is called on to recognize departments and at times he calls the entire roll asking each director or outreach leader to report the number of persons who are present to visit for their department. When a department is well represented the pastor will ask the entire group to stand and others will applaud. Some of our departments may be competing with other departments to see who has the most visitors out. This is especially true in the youth age range. Special visitation report chalkboards have been provided for each age division. Each board includes the name of the department, the director, department outreach leader, and a space where the number attending the supper can be recorded.

This report may be secured by having the Sunday School outreach director or someone else posted at the entrance of the dining room or at the cashier's table so that he can ask each person which department he represents. Before the promotion meeting begins, the number of visitors can be posted on the report boards. The pastor calls out the figures of outstanding groups or he might mention all departments.

At times one or two persons give a testimony of a successful visitation experience. These are brief and to the point. From time to time a brief demonstration is presented showing how to present the plan of salvation or how to visit a newcomer or an absentee. Again it must be emphasized that great care is taken to get the people out of the buildings and into the homes for visitation. Brochures, maps and other visitation materials are provided in a convenient place, and visitors are encouraged to leave something in each home.

The promotional meeting is closed on a spiritual note. Visitors are challenged to be faithful witnesses presenting the claims of Christ to the best of their ability and to depend upon the Holy Spirit to use their efforts. They are reminded of the victories the church is experiencing in reaching people. Illustrations are given of how someone's life has been changed because they were reached through visitation. It is helpful to tell of examples of how whole families have been reached or how a little girl or boy has been won to Christ. Meetings always close with prayer. One or two verses of a song or chorus might be used to begin the meeting or just before the closing prayer.

Assigning the Prospects

Prospects are usually assigned ahead of time. In many churches it is common to see visitors waste fifteen to thirty minutes waiting for an assignment or trying to decide which prospect to visit. Our department directors or outreach leaders make assignments on Sunday during the Sunday School hour. Some who may not be able to come to the church on visitation night can make their visits at other times.

Names of new prospects who visited the previous Sunday or newcomers are passed out to department outreach leaders or directors at the door of the dining room on visitation night. Our general outreach director will have a few prospect assignments available in case department leaders are absent or otherwise are unable to make the assignment. It is best not to display these prospects on a general assignment board. Prospect assignments should be made to the department director or outreach leader and they need to feel the responsibility for being present to make assignments to their department visitors. Key prospects, however, may be assigned by mail or by calling certain people in the congregation who are felt to have a particular capacity for reaching a given prospect.

Keeping Prospect Information Up to Date

Experience has shown that the postman is probably the greatest single helper in keeping prospect information current. About four years ago the prospect file at Travis Avenue was put on addressoplates. This made it possible to mail promotional information concerning revivals or special music programs to prospects. Each time a mailout is sent, the two words "Return Requested" are written under the return address in the upper left hand corner of the envelope. The post office returns the undelivered cards or letters to us with the change of address if it is available. The result of our first mailout was astounding. We sent letters out to approximately one thousand prospect families. The postman literally brought back hundreds of these letters which he could not deliver. Over three hundred prospect families were eliminated because they had moved from the city. Many others had moved to different addresses within the city. When everything was completely corrected, rather than having one thousand families in the prospect file, we had approximately seven hundred families. Many of the seven hundred families, however, also had moved and the postman had given us their new and now correct address. For each letter that was returned we had to pay the postman ten cents. Perhaps this is the best money we spend to help keep an up-to-date prospect file.

In order to keep our file as current as possible now, prospects receive mailouts during the revival preparation time so that we can update our information just before a revival. At Christmas time they may be invited to attend the church music program. In the summer they are invited to Vacation Bible School or to begin a new year in Bible study in the fall. Each of these emphases not only inform and invite people but *serve to correct our file.*

Before we began this practice, at least one out of every three prospects in our file had an incorrect address or did not even live in the city. No wonder church members become discouraged and do not like to visit.

A second important way to keep the file accurate is to ask for reports. This seems to be a great undertaking in most of our churches. We have to continually sell the value of reporting visits. Reports can often save other workers a great amount of time spent in useless efforts of visitation. Our members are urged to turn in reports or to call the church office to tell that a family has moved, or that information is incorrect. Make every effort to let it be known that the prospect file is being updated continually for the benefit of all who visit.

Building a Prospect File

A question very often asked is, "Where do you get your prospects?" This has not been a big problem in our visitation work at Travis. Of course the best prospects that we have are those who visit the Sunday School or worship services. Visitors are asked to fill out cards in the Sunday School and worship services. These are typed up and assigned to Sunday School departments on each week.

Another good source for prospects is the newcomer service. Most cities have some kind of a Welcome Wagon or a newcomer service which will supply the church with the names and addresses, and often the religious preference, of new people moving into the city. In other cities the local papers publish the names and addresses of new water meter or gas meter connections. These can be followed up and contacted to find their religious preference.

Another good method of securing good prospects is from members of the church. From time to time department directors ask members to give names and addresses of persons they know at work or in their neighborhood who need to be reached by the church.

Another good source of securing prospect information that we have used at Travis has been that of having outreach spectaculars. Some special event is planned which has attraction to people beyond our local church membership and to the secular world. These activities are advertised in the city papers and sometimes on radio. As people attend the services, everyone, including the members, are asked to register. Some who attend are unsaved, or are unaffiliated Baptists looking for a church home.

Another fruitful source of prospect information is the telephone survey. Practice has shown that it is often wise to take a small area of the city and to get only information that is absolutely necessary to determine that prospects live in a home. A follow-up visit is made to the home to get information about each member of the family. Persons making the survey will not spend as much time on the telephone

```
Wade, Mr. & Mrs. Wm. C.                    NC 1-26-71
4515 Evans        76115                    Med. Ad. 1




Also:  Julie        Senior 2
       Pam          Senior 1
       Henry        Student Career
```

and therefore can call more families in a shorter period of time. A sample card is shown.

Another source is a door to door canvass. It may be conducted in the same way as the telephone survey, getting only essential information which can be followed up on later.

One of the best ways that we have discovered prospects has been through our Vacation Bible School pre-enrolment plan. This is discussed in detail in the chapter on Vacation Bible School. In brief, however, we make block assignments and members go door to door pre-enrolling boys and girls for Vacation Bible School. Then following Vacation Bible School each family is assigned to the Sunday School for follow-up and visitation. Literally hundreds of prospects are discovered each year.

Organizing the Prospect File

Two files are needed for an effective system: one alphabetical file for family units and a file set up by Sunday School departments. The

```
                    Department File

                       Class File

                      Office File
                PROSPECT VISITATION ASSIGNMENT
Name _____ Date _____
      (if under 17 yrs., give parents name _____

Address _____ Phone _____

Date of Birth or Age _____

Christian? _____ Church Member? _____
What Church? _____

Special Information for Visitor _____
_____

Source of Information _____

PLEASE:  (1)  Report information after visit on pink Visitation
              Report Slips.
         (2)  Report on pink slips who else should visit: Youth,
              Pastor, Superintendent, etc.
```

family file has a separate card for each family. The name of each family member is listed on the card along with the Sunday School department the person is assigned to. This file serves as a control file for the Sunday School department.

The Sunday School file is made up by individual names and are divided by departments according to age or school grade.

Visitation assignments are made on a regular triplicate form. One copy marked "office copy" is placed in the department file which is kept in the office. Two other copies are then given the department. One of these goes to the department outreach leader and the other goes to the class outreach leader. In the children's division the department outreach leader gets both copies and simply uses the extra copy for assignment purposes.

Each department outreach leader is encouraged to keep a prospect file. Many use a file box designed for 4 by 6-inch cards. These are supplied to each department upon request. Department leaders work out their own assignments.

Training for Visitation

Some training needs to be done to improve the quality of visitation. At Travis we have had on various occasions evangelistic institutes or training in personal witnessing aimed at reaching the unsaved person. This takes place on one, two or three nights of a given week. Also courses are offered on personal witnessing and general visitation on Sunday night during the church training hour.

One of the most helpful times to train visitors is at the visitation supper. One key point can be made just before persons go out to visit. Care should be taken, however, not to take too much time so that the people can get on out of the buildings and into the homes. It is also practical to send an inexperienced visitor with one who has good experience. This is probably the most useful and practical approach churches can utilize.

Leave Something in the Home

Very often in a metropolitan area visitors go out without any printed material or information about the church. Prospects need to have some way to distinguish between churches. Certainly an impression needs to be left about what denomination or what church actually is expressing the interest in them. This can be done with a brochure or by leaving a copy of a recent church paper. In addition to a church promotion item, tracts are often helpful to leave with lost persons or others not familiar with Southern Baptists. A brochure, door hanger, or card left at the home can at least let the person know that a church is interested in him.

Greet Prospects When They Come

As prospects enter the buildings for Sunday School and worship they need to receive a warm welcome. Our church has a greeter committee, and greeters are posted near the main entrance where most people enter for Sunday School. Greeters meet prospects with a smile and take them to a nearby room where they can be seated at tables to fill in a visitor registration slip. When these slips are completed on each member of the family, the members are classified and are escorted to the department of their age group. Usually the youngest member of the family is taken to his department first so that other family members can know where he will be. Then the next youngest, etc. is taken one after another until finally the mother and dad are taken to their department. In each instance the department outreach leader or someone else is assigned to greet all new people as they are brought to the department. This is an important aspect of the work which gives a good first impression which is so important. A church will either be considered friendly or unfriendly depending on what happens in those early moments when new people come for Sunday School or worship.

At the worship services, of course, the ushers greet the people at the door. During the service one of the staff members greets the visitors and has them stand while the ushers present them with a visitor's packet. They are asked to fill out the card, to pin a ribbon to their clothing, and to drop the card in the offering plate when it is passed. This not only recognizes the visitors, it gives our church members a chance to see where the visitors are seated, and supplies important prospect information which is used for follow up later.

Visitation Revival

Every church would do well to have a visitation revival at least once. At Travis Avenue we have had two visitation revivals in the last four years. Prospect assignments are made and each Sunday School department is called on to visit each night, Monday through Friday for an entire week. Supper is served at 6 o'clock each night following a brief word of instruction and members go out to visit all over the city. At 8:30 P.M. a report snack is held back at the church where people report the results of the visits they have made. A large report board is used to record the results of each department's efforts. Competition is established between departments in an effort to visit all known prospects and to reach new members.

It was interesting to note that our young people became tremendously interested and involved in both visitation revivals and were able to reach a number of unchurched youth. Visits were recorded only when reports were turned in. It seems that the emphasis of such a revival should be placed upon the number of persons visiting, the number of visits made, and the number of persons reached rather than upon how many visits are made.

All churches could benefit by having one visitation revival to establish their visitation program, to train persons in visitation, to bring prospect information up to date, to communicate the value of the visitation report, and above all, to reach unchurched persons.

CHAPTER IV
ESTABLISHING ATTENDANCE GOALS

At the onset of this book, it needs to be stated that the purpose of it all, the purpose of our study, the purpose of our changes, all of it was with the overall goal in mind—to *reach more people for our Lord and for study in his Word.* The reader might say, then your emphasis is majoring on numbers. If you want to word it that way, you may. We prefer to call it reaching people, reaching souls, reaching out, harvesting people for the Lord, as he commanded us to do.

In recent years we have de-emphasized numbers in our churches. Many churches which formerly stated statistics in their church bulletins, do not do so any longer. True, there is danger in becoming enamoured by statistics. Yet, when we keep in mind that each number represents a soul, it keeps numbers in proper perspective. Usually, when we "play down" numbers, it means we have no number in our churches to which we wish to call attention. We aren't doing much, so we'd rather not broadcast it.

People are still out there! They are still needing to be reached. They need the Lord. They need the influence of the church. They need Bible study. They need to know that God said to "remember his day"—"to study"—"to assemble together."

They are everywhere. They are members of our churches who are not active. They are unaffiliated Baptists. They are unsaved. They are disinterested. They are lonely. They are prosperous. They are poor. They are young. They are old. On and on we could go. But they all have a common denominator. It is a need for a meaning, a purpose, a goal in life. In short, they all need the saving power of Jesus Christ and his meaning of life injected into their souls.

How can we reach them? What can our churches do that we are not doing? One thing we found among these churches who are reaching people—*they are setting goals.* They are majoring on attendance. Attendance is the desired end and so goals become one of the means to that desired end.

Actually we have learned this from the secular world as well. They set goals in the business world and keep these goals before their salesmen and keep reminding them what they are seeking to accomplish. Corporation management studies have shown that this method works; it motivates and it inspires. Also their studies show us that it is best to have only one or two major goals, seldom more than three or four. If goals are set in too many areas, priority of effort is lost.

In our exploration of means used by other churches it was immediately obvious that most of the large, growing churches not only focused their attention upon attendance but upon attendance on "the Lord's Day." It seems that the efforts and energies of our people in our busy society can be focused only upon one *major emphasis* during the week. Other emphases are good, to be sure, but we observed that where the emphasis is placed upon Sunday and the efforts are being made to get people to attend on *that day* great numbers are being reached. Many churches which have weekday ministries find their overall attendance to be declining. This may be a temporary situation, but one wonders if a lack of focus is responsible. In summary it seems evident that attendance can be increased more easily when we focus toward the time when most people can attend. That time continues to be Sunday, at least for the present.

Now with these introductory thoughts in mind, let's seek to explore in depth the use of attendance goals. We want to limit our goals to the most essential emphases.

For instance, some of the following might be chosen. Attendance, new members, persons reporting visits, or persons attending teachers and officers meeting. Goals set in these four areas ask for results. If we add to these another six or eight emphases, we lose much of the value because our sense of priority tends to be lost.

The following suggestions are offered. Meet with all leaders involved and ask them to help set individual goals for their classes or departments. In larger churches this may be a meeting of Sunday School department directors and outreach leaders. In smaller churches it would involve department directors, teachers, and all class and department outreach leaders.

The second step in setting goals is to ask the department or class leaders to set goals for their group and then to report that goal to the entire group of Sunday School leaders. The general Sunday School outreach director should call the roll of each department or class. Each department or class representative answers the roll by giving the goal for his group. Each goal is written down as it is given. When all have reported, the grand total is announced to the entire group. Very often in our meetings with department directors and outreach leaders someone will offer to raise his goal to help round off the overall goal to an even fifty or an even one hundred. The climate of such a meeting produces an enthusiastic spirit of interest and also a little healthy competition.

Following this a discussion of how to reach these goals is helpful. Various persons are asked for suggestions as to how he or she might be able to lead his department or class to reach its goal. As suggestions are offered, every leader is listening. Many ideas will be presented which will prove helpful to others in the group. Sometimes it is helpful to have a general promotional approach which all departments will use. The important thing, however, is that each class or department has a definite plan to help reach its own goal. Not only is it important for them to set their goal, it is also important for them to choose their own way of reaching it.

We have had good experience at Travis Avenue with *setting annual goals* for attendance. The idea is for each department to set a goal that it hopes to be averaging by the end of the year. This does not mean that they will average the goal for the entire twelve months. For example, three years ago average goals were set by our departments which came to a grand total of sixteen hundred for the entire Sunday School. This meant that if all departments reached their average attendance goal the Sunday School would average sixteen hundred. Later goals were set to average eighteen hundred in Sunday School. A year later goals were set to average two thousand in Sunday School attendance. By the time this book is printed goals are likely to be set to average twenty-two hundred or better because each time they have been set they have been reached. This does not mean that every department reaches its goal. Some do and some do not, but all departments have before them a goal which is a constant reminder of the progress they expect to make. This is also carried through to each class in all youth and adult departments. Every group is oriented to strive to reach an outreach goal. With all groups working toward their goals, all make a contribution to the total goal.

These overall goals—the monthly goals, annual goals, etc.—are kept before the people by listing them in the mid-week promotion sheet. Attention is called to them each week, thus interest stays alive. Comparison is made between goals and actual achievement and how we are progressing toward our goals. Those departments reaching their goals are indicated by an asterisk. See the sample promotion sheet.

Two or three times throughout the year special high attendance

61 Establishing Attendance Goals

MID-WEEK TAB - - - - S.S. Report for Sunday, April 18, 1971

Dept./Dir./ORL	Attendance	2000 Goal	2500 Goal	NM	Offering	Visitation Supper
G.O./Hutchison/Johnson	39****	30	37	-	181.69	8
Sr.Ad.2/Gollnick/Gr./Ch.	135**	150	165	1	414.00	8
Sr.Ad.1/Millican/Loyd	147***	156	195	-	1505.57	
Med.Ad.3/Rigby/Goodell	106*****	96	120	-	824.00	3
Med.Ad.2/Brooks/Isham	91*	95	120	-	767.50	-
Med.Ad.1/Hedrick/Bunzendahl	59	80	100	-	573.96	5
Y.Ad.2/Aleman/Briggs	63	72	82	1	409.00	5
Y.Ad.1/Wadsworth/Pennington	53	65	82	-	553.24	6
Single Bus.&P./Stewart/Melton	17	35	45	-	107.75	4
MYP/Dowdy/Sammons	69**	75	106	-	450.70	14
Totals - Adult	740	824	1015	2	5605.72	51
S/C/Kelly/Holt	95***	90	112	3	236.45	16
Sr.3/Morgan/Taylor	24*	31	35	-	98.95	4
Sr.2/Sikes/Wiley	56**	53	66	-	190.09	10
Sr.1/English/Haggard	37*	38	48	-	213.00	3
Int.3/Hardin/Brooks	47	55	63	1	45.84	23
Int.2/Bailey/	45**	44	55	1	84.19	2
Int.1/York/Briggs	71***	60	72	1	322.71	12
Totals - Youth	375*	371	451	6	1191.23	70
6th Gr B/Leitch/Hughes	15	28	28	-	40.20	1
6th Gr A/Jetton/Hughes	57	70	70	1	107.44	1
5th Gr/Collins/Hightower	59	76	86	-	284.43	3
4th Gr B/Smith/Sanders	36****	35	40	-	24.04	-
4th Gr A/Strickling/Clayton	43**	43	54	-	199.98	1
3rd Gr C/Lee/Salter	31***	28	35	-	28.75	-
3rd Gr B/Kuhlman/Malone	23*	28	28	2	12.00	-
3rd Gr A/Cardwell/Miller	29	35	35	-	15.81	-
2nd Gr D/	22	-	13	-	23.60	-
2nd Gr C/Blanchard/Borden	24*	30	30	-	40.15	-
2nd Gr B/Andrews/	27***	30	35	-	36.35	1
2nd Gr A/Yost/Walton	27	36	27	1	52.05	-
1st Gr D/	14	-	13	-	11.56	-
1st Gr C/Yockstick/Bumpas	25*	30	30	-	51.00	-
1st Gr B/Pinter/	23	26	27	-	16.40	-
1st Gr A/Butner/	20**	25	30	-	17.70	-
Totals - Children	475	520	555	4	961.46	7
PS C-9/Whitaker/Whitaker	24*****	20	28	-	9.22	1
PS C-7/Greene/	21	-	26	-	55.57	1
PS C-6/Dwight/Berger	21***	20	23	-	66.87	-
PS C-5/Baker/Trawick	20*****	20	25	-	11.70	-
PS C-4/Williams/Lane	24**	18	20	-	56.42	-
PS C-3/Wood/	13	15	15	-	.99	-
PS C-2/Grant/Eubanks	19*	22	25	-	53.16	-
PS C-1/Neill/Sikes	15	20	23	-	35.45	-
PS TOTALS - Beginner	157****	135	185	-	289.38	2
PS B-5/Miller/	18**	19	22	-	26.71	-
PS B-4/McQuade/Bell	23****	15	16	-	21.63	-
PS B-3/Doyle/Hedquist	16*****	16	18	-	93.66	1
PS B-2/Rice/Pearson	20*****	20	16	-	1.83	-
PS B-1/Litzler/Lietzler	13***	12	12	-	15.96	-
PS A-6/Jackson/	6****	8	8	-	-	-
PS A-5/Kolls/Kolls	14**	15	17	-	10.20	-
PS A-4/Nance/	12*****	11	11	-	20.30	-
Baby 1-2-3/Ward/Cald./Pat.	35****	30	32	-	35.35	-
Special Ed./Holt	13****	11	13	-	44.75	2
PS Totals - Nursery	170	157	162	-	270.39	3
Deaf, Youth Away & Others	33**	-	24	-	46.25	-
TOTALS - - - - - -	1989	2008	2432	12	8546.11	141

2500

SUNDAY is the day to have 2500 in Sunday School. As we do this we will be the #2 Sunday School in the more than 34,000 Southern Baptist churches.

DON'T TOUCH YOUR CLOCK.

We will have Sunday School and worship on Central Standard Time and will have a "Time Changing Ceremony" during the worship service.

Bring an apple for your teacher Sunday for Teacher Appreciation Day.

days are promoted. Two of these are usually scheduled on the Sundays following our spring and fall revivals. Previously we set goals for the closing Sunday of revivals. This great climactic day usually was followed by a day of poor attendance, but by waiting a week after revival services conclude, we overcome the let down usually experienced. The spirit of revival continues for a second week and we do not experience a letdown which usually follows a revival. Below are listed the experience of our last five revivals. The first two columns show the results of setting high attendance on the last Sunday of the revival while the last three show the results of high attendance on the Sunday one week following the revival:

	Spring 1968	*Fall* 1969	*Spring* 1970	*Fall* 1970	*Spring* 1971
Sunday Before Revival	1629	1584	1746	1815	1923
First Sunday of Revival	1635	1591	1728	1885	2005
Last Sunday of Revival	1690	1817	1789	1913	1989
Sunday After Revival	1506	1399**	2003	2209	2348
2nd Sunday After Revival	1368	1541	1753	1726	1934

** Time Change

In addition to the numerical progress shown on the chart the spirit of our workers and others continues to be high. This is perhaps the greatest benefit of all.

An alternate plan for goal setting may be to build around a percent of increase over existing attendance averages. For example, the average attendance of each department for a recent five- or six-week period might be compiled. The goal setting planning sheet could be prepared such as the one shown above. With the average attendance figures in mind, discussion would center upon an overall attendance increase. If the group agreed to a 10 percent increase, all groups would then figure their goal based upon that percentage. This method is useful and yet seems to be less desirable than the approach above. Where there is less involvement, there is less commitment—as in all of life.

If other goals are to be set, columns are provided in the goal setting plan sheet. Various emphases need to be highlighted at various times, such as number of new members to be reached, the number of persons visiting in behalf of a department, and the number of workers attending officers and teachers meeting each week. Again it should be noted that goals should be as few in number as possible.

Goals Deal with Results

Please note that the goals discussed above relate primarily to the actual results desired of the Sunday School. In the past we have spent a great deal of time talking about things that are important but which are actually more of a means to an end rather than the results desired. For example, we formerly emphasized the number of visits reported by each class and department. When we first began using goals, two to three hundred visits were being reported by our people each week. To increase our visitation efforts goals were set by classes and departments. Within two years we were reporting six to eight hundred visits each week and sometimes even higher.

Certainly we saw an increase in the number of persons being reached by the church, but we did not see an increase in proportion to the number of visits being made. We found that because of the numerous visits being made some prospects were becoming intimidated. As the emphasis was placed upon the number of visits the quality of visits decreased. Later we learned that it would be best to emphasize the *number of persons who actually made visits* rather than the number of visits being made. This has done much to improve the quality of the visits and to give more purposefulness to our work. Visitors enter a home relaxed and do a better job. It is better to make two or three good calls than to make six or seven hurried ones.

It is really more important that people be reached than it is to visit them. Visitation is a means to an end. We visit to reach. Goals need to be set for new members and for the number of workers who go to visit. Our goals are set to help increase the work force (visitors), to reach people (new members), to get people into Bible study (attendance), and to improve the quality of work (teachers and officers' meeting attendance).

High Attendance Days

It seems that high attendance days should not be set too often. For one thing, if they are, they become less effective. We are convinced that the basic annual goal for attendance increase is of greater importance. Perhaps two or three special high attendance days is ample. Certainly one each quarter of the year is enough.

Again it seems best for these emphases to be set up on a departmental basis rather than on the general Sunday School level. Departmental plans often have a greater lasting effect on the department and are certainly better understood and accepted by department workers and members. These, however, are to be done in coordination with general Sunday School plans.

The emphasis on high attendance days centers around reaching the absentees and key prospects. During the week following these special days, absentees and prospects are again emphasized so that permanent results can be realized.

For the past two years goals have been set in the spring of a series of weeks. In 1970 a special series of five Sunday School lessons were chosen for each age group out of their regular Sunday School lesson materials. They were emphasized by their content. Members and prospects were challenged to be in at least four of the five lessons for this period of time. They were encouraged to sign the card and to turn it in as a pledge of their attendance. The left side of the card was retained as a reminder of their pledge. These lessons gave meaning to an emphasis upon attendance.

During this five-week period we were making an effort to reach our "1800" goals (these were the annual department goals set earlier which totaled 1800) or to average 1800 in attendance. The last Sunday was to be a special high attendance day or a catch-up day for

Establishing Attendance Goals

```
         SUNDAY SCHOOL LESSONS                    |     I'll Be There
Adults-12th Grade                                 |
Mar. 15 "Living Under Human Authority" (Rom. 13:1-7; I Pet.
                                    2:11-17)      |
Mar. 22 "The Christian's Influence" (Rom. 14:1-23)|        John Q. Doe
Mar. 29 "Risen With Christ" (Col. 2:6-3:17)       |        2800 Your Street
Apr. 5  "Christ, the Christian's Example" (Rom. 15)|       Ft. Worth, Texas
Apr. 12 "Helpers or Hinderers" (Rom. 16)          |
                                                  |
8th-11th Grades                                   |
Lessons on the Holy Spirit and on God the Son     |
                                              CUT |  Believing in the value of Bible Study and Worship and
7th Grade                                     HERE|  Desiring to see Christ's Church be victorious in these
The Doctrine of Salvation and The Doctrine of the Church  days . . .
                                                  |
4th-6th Grades                                    |    I'll be there for Sunday School at least 4 out of 5
Peter and His Deep Faith in Christ (Preacher, Healer, and  Sundays, March 15-April 12 (especially April 12) unless I
Missionary) and Learning More About God From Jesus  am providentially hindered due to illness, work responsi-
                                                    bility, etc.
1st-3rd Grades
Paul and His Missionary Activities and The Church Now and
in Bible Days                                       Signed  John Q. Doe

4 and 5 Year Olds
The Best Book and The World God Made

Nursery
God Loves Me and God's Outdoor Wonders
```

the entire campaign. As it turned out, we needed to have 2003 present to reach our 1800 average. This was reached and proved to us again the value of goals. This goal was reached on the Sunday one week following the close of our spring revival.

In the spring of 1971 a goal of two thousand was set for a six-week period which also climaxed on the Sunday one week following the close of the revival. The two thousand goal was reached during the first five weeks of the emphasis, but we still planned to have a special high attendance emphasis on the last week of the six-week period.

High attendance days can be built around special lessons, teacher appreciation, the use of a commitment card for a given day, or a special assembly during department periods in adult and youth age groups.

Two illustrations of the above are found below. In the spring of 1971 it was decided that we would reach for the second highest attendance in the Southern Baptist Convention on a given Sunday. It was felt that if our goal was reached that only the First Baptist Church of Dallas would have a higher attendance on that day in the local Sunday School. So, therefore, Travis would be *number two*. The emphasis was to push to be number two. Our people responded in a good spirit and with the cooperation of the Avis Rent-a-Car Company, buttons were secured—"We Try Harder" buttons. The company was most cooperative in providing them and as was mentioned our people responded in good fashion. Another idea which has been used for teacher appreciation day is that of "Bring your teacher an apple on teacher appreciation day." Again it is a simple idea and many teachers received bright shiny apples from their pupils which made for building good spirit and also brought a lot of fun into Sunday School classes. One department superintendent received an apple pie.

We have been careful to avoid the giving of prizes or gifts of any monetary value as a motivation for high attendance. We simply rely upon the class organization and the emphasis within the department to accomplish these goals. Cards, telephone calls, visits, and effort such as this are the primary means used to accomplish any attendance or other goals.

CHAPTER V
BUS MINISTRY

Why have a bus ministry? Perhaps the greatest single reason for having a bus ministry lies in its potential for *evangelistic outreach*—witnessing to the saving power of Jesus Christ to those around us. On the first Sunday our very first bus ran, a thirteen-year-old girl made her profession of faith in Christ. By the end of the first year of a bus ministry at Travis Avenue Baptist Church more than 250 boys, girls, and adult riders had presented themselves on profession of faith in Christ and united with our church.

As the young people and adults ride the buses, they are oriented into spiritual matters. They become acquainted with the Bible which many have seen for the very first time. Soon they are presented with their own copy of a New Testament—such as *Good News For Modern Man*.

One child excitedly took her copy home and showed it to her mother. Over a period of time the mother, reading the book of John, accepted Jesus as her Savior. Then she shared this experience with her husband. Soon an entire family of nine trusted the Lord and later made public these decisions. This happens often with the people who ride our buses.

This ministry is a concrete means of demonstrating our spiritual concern. It is definitely another evangelistic arm reaching out in service to those around us. It is not at all uncommon to have entire families professing our Lord publicly after interested workers have won them to faith in Christ.

Out of this spiritual ministry comes another reason for a bus ministry—an *opportunity to show social concern*. At first we observed that some people do not feel free to come to church because of improper clothing, lack of Bible knowledge, or other such reason. However, after continued interest and visits on the part of the bus workers, this economic and educational barrier is broken down. As the ministry is continued and as the children get into a regular routine of Sunday School attendance, parents begin to realize that our church is truly interested in their family.

Often there is a real evident need for tangible expressions of concern. These needs have been met, also. Clothing, food, and other items have been provided over and over again. (This will be discussed further later on in the chapter.)

Perhaps one of the most rewarding reasons for a bus ministry is to *reach children of unconcerned parents*. Oh, how very many adults are indifferent to their own spiritual needs and likewise to the spiritual needs of their children. Formerly we visited these people, the children showed an interest, but could or did not attend because their parents would not bring them. With a bus going by their home for them, they can attend without parents—but in most cases, with the approval of the parents. Children respond to the love and interest of concerned workers. Hundreds who never had been inside a church now call Travis "my church."

Also, a bus ministry reaches *senior adults and others* who desire to come but have no transportation. Many are dependent upon others but prefer to be independent. Having a bus come to their door solves this problem for them. Senior adults who live in downtown hotels and apartment complexes are so gratified to have transportation to church.

The last reason we will mention for having a bus ministry is the *opportunity* it gives to church members *to render service*. Never have we had so many people working, so many people developing as soul-winners, so many people rendering service as we have had since our bus ministry began. One worker said, "All my life as a Christian I had prayed that I could be a soul-winner. Now I am really winning people." More people are rending personal service in tangible ways —providing clothing, food, even refrigerators and other home needs. More people are teaching children, more people are learning to love, to care, to be more interested in others than they are in themselves. On and on we could go, listing reasons for a bus ministry.

How to Begin a Bus Ministry

Study Your Community

In some areas churches can begin a bus ministry right in their very own neighborhood. In other areas it might be necessary to spread on out. Look for sections cut off from the main residential districts by railroad tracks or small industries. Look for apartment complexes or trailer courts. Look for areas where large numbers of people live; children's homes, geriatric homes, military bases.

Enlist Riders

Our church has used two methods successfully to enlist boys, girls, and adults for the buses. The Sunday School workers have done the canvassing; also, bus captains and crew members have done the canvassing.

Sunday School Canvass

Of course, this is done very much as any other door-to-door canvassing. We determine how many blocks will be surveyed; then divide the blocks among the Sunday School departments. Usually it takes each canvasser about one hour to complete a block.

It is the responsibility of the departments and class leaders to get their assigned blocks canvassed. Brief training sessions are held during Sunday morning assemblies, as a Sunday noon luncheon, or at regular visitation suppers. Canvassers get a full explanation of the purpose of the canvassing, the area assigned, and a suggested approach to the occupants—perhaps in a "how to" and "how not to" demonstration. Materials used for the canvass will be discussed later.

The suggested conversation we have used is as follows:

"I am from Travis Avenue Baptist Church. We are locating families in this area who are interested in riding a bus to Sunday School and worship services. We are chartering a city bus which will come to your front door every Sunday morning around 9:00 o'clock and will take you to Sunday School and worship and will return you to your home around noon. Are there members of your family who would like for the bus to stop for them?"

If the family indicates an interest one of the cards below is filled out:

```
                    BUS OUTREACH INFORMATION
    Family Name_____

    Address_____

    Telephone_____

    List those to ride the bus:

    Name_____Birthdate_____Grade_____

    Name_____Birthdate_____Grade_____

    Name_____Birthdate_____Grade_____

    Name_____Birthdate_____Grade_____

    Name_____Birthdate_____Grade_____
```

Experience has shown that when approximately one hundred average size blocks are canvassed we can expect to locate about thirty families with some interest in riding a bus. Many canvasses will pre-enrol no one. It is, therefore, important that workers know this before they go so they will not be disappointed. Each is to do his best as he surveys his block, knowing he will share in the success of the overall effort.

When the canvassing is completed, compiled, and processed, each home is plotted on a map and the route is organized. The bus crew then returns to each home on the Saturday before the bus is to run the first day. They visit with parents and children to further discuss the schedule. All members of the family are encouraged to ride.

If the canvassers and bus crew do their jobs well, it is likely that there will be from ten to twenty-five people riding on the first Sunday. The second Sunday may drop off in attendance, but in the next two or three months the bus is likely to be reaching from thirty-five to forty-five persons each week.

Bus Crew Canvass

This canvassing is done in the same way as the Sunday School canvass discussed above. The difference is that the bus crew does all of the work, requiring a great deal more effort on the part of a few workers.

The Sunday School canvassing has the advantage of covering more territory more quickly and thus getting the bus off to a better start. It also helps a larger cross section of the membership feel that they have a part in this ministry. These Sunday School members find the prospects and then the bus crew cultivates and reaches them. Furthermore, the bus workers will locate new riders almost every week. There is a constant relocation of riders; somt moving out, others in.

How to Secure the Buses

There are a number of ways to secure buses. Perhaps the simplest way to get started is to rent them. Many cities have their own transit systems and rent their buses on an hourly basis. Using city buses has many advantages. In most instances they can be chartered or cancelled on short notice. Parents have more confidence in the safety of their children when they see a uniformed driver in the city transit bus. The rental price includes insurance and driver as well as use of the bus.

It is possible to rent buses from other sources. Some Catholic school parent organizations purchase buses to transport their children to their own schools. They will sometimes rent them on Sundays for a minimal amount. It will probably be necessary to furnish drivers and to provide insurance. They would of course maintain the buses. Still others may be rented from individuals who have contracts with public school districts. Many own and operate their own buses.

The outstanding advantage of renting buses is that the church can major on outreach and can secure the energies of others to provide the transportation for the ministry. The problems of driver training, maintenance, insurance, security against vandalism, and the initial outlay of funds to purchase equipment must be considered. These responsibilities alone will take much time and forethought and may call for an additional church staff member very early in the ministry.

Many churches, however, choose to own their buses. Certainly, this approach should be thoroughly considered by all. Perhaps it would be wise to rent buses until the ministry is established. This would give leaders a chance to discover the potential and limitations of the ministry without fully committing themselves to the full responsibilities of bus ownership.

Buses being used by churches throughout the nation range from old school buses purchased for $300 to $400 each to some of the most modern equipment available which costs as much as $40,000 to $50,000 each. Many churches buy school buses which are six to ten years old. In recent months the price for such buses has increased significantly. Some have full time bus ministers and employ one or more mechanics. Most take their equipment to a repair shop or get members to volunteer their services to maintain it. Some maintain a spare bus in case of a break down.

A key advantage of owning buses is to have them for many uses in the life of the church. Churches intending to provide transportation for all services would certainly need to consider the purchase of buses.

How To Secure Workers

Workers, of course, must be sought to build this work. Some members of the congregation will emerge to serve in the bus ministry who have never served in any other way. The following suggestions are offered:

1. Take a survey through the Sunday School or in a worship service and ask people to indicate their possible interest in working with the bus ministry.

2. Look for men who visit regularly or who bring persons to church in their own cars.

3. Keep the bus ministry constantly before the congregation. Recognize the bus captains and workers for outstanding accomplishments.

4. Choose captains for new routes from the outreach visitors on routes already established.

5. Study the Sunday School rolls for names of men who are faithful in attendance and visitation. Visit in their homes to lay the challenge before them.

6. Have workers and riders give testimonies about the work.

How to Organize the Workers

The bus ministry requires a dedicated group of effective workers. They must be willing to visit their riders and to seek new ones each week. They need to be compassionate in order to minister to indifferent parents, undisciplined children, and human tragedy. Only those who have a commitment to this work will be effective.

What workers are needed? Different approaches may be taken. Some churches select a director to be in charge of the entire ministry, a bus pastor or captain to be in charge of each bus, and a driver for each bus. Others have a director, captain or pastor, group leaders, game and song leaders, drivers, and a general secretary.

Let's discuss briefly the work of each of these persons.

1. *The bus director.*—This person may be responsible to the pastor, the minister of education, or to a bus ministry committee.

His ministry would primarily include:

(1) Determine the need for new routes and determine the boundaries of all routes.

(2) Lead out in the establishing of new routes.

(3) Help develop procedures for handling the riders on the bus, at church, and at other times.

(4) Enlist and train workers.

(5) Develop and improve a bus record system. (See forms.)

(6) Deal with any problems related to the ministry.

(7) Work to relate the bus ministry to the Sunday School and the rest of the church program.

(8) Secure and maintain the buses.

(9) Make recommendations for the bus budget.

(10) Lead in promoting attendance on each bus.

2. *The bus captain.*—Duties of each bus captain would include the following:

(1) Plan, conduct, and evaluate the outreach and transportation ministry of his assigned route.

(2) Enlist outreach visitors to visit riders and prospective riders.

(3) Adjust route and schedule to meet the needs of his riders.

(4) Direct the driver over the route.

(5) See that his bus record book is checked and report the results of work each Sunday.

(6) See that the church name or sign is properly displayed on the bus.

(7) See that all passengers are returned home and that children are returned to the custody of their parents or guardian.

(8) Develop good public relations for the church.

(9) See that each rider and prospect is assigned to an outreach visitor for visitation, cultivation, and watch care.

(10) See that appropriate discipline is maintained on the bus at all times.

(11) Attend the bus workers planning meeting every Saturday morning at 9:00 A.M.

(12) Hold planning meeting with outreach visitors as necessary.

(13) See that each child is identified when he gets on the bus. (The method we use is placing a name tag on each rider; stamping his hand with identification of assigned department.)

(14) Plan special activities for riders throughout the year.

3. *Bus outreach visitor.*—Duties of this person would include the following:

(1) Visit an assigned group of riders each Saturday.

(2) Always "look out" for new riders to enlist.

(3) Assist with records, discipline, refreshments, signs, loading and unloading of passengers each Sunday.

(4) Develop good public relations for the church.

(5) Attend the bus workers planning meeting every Saturday morning at 9:00 o'clock.

(6) Check to be sure that each rider in the group is accounted for each Sunday.

(7) Minister to the entire family of each rider on the assigned group.

4. *The bus driver.*—The driver is responsible to drive the bus as directed by the bus captain. He will look out for the safety of the group by driving carefully and by seeing that his bus is road safe. He should be properly licensed and should assist the captain as needed.

5. *The bus secretary.*—The secretary prepares a general report of *all buses each Sunday* morning. This person assists the bus captains with their records and maintains an office record book for each bus

route. He works with each bus captain to maintain a record card on each rider and checks his attendance each week.

6. *The game and song leader.*—This individual helps make the best use of the time riders spend on the bus by doing the following:

(1) Lead in singing songs which will prepare riders for Sunday School and will help them enjoy the time they are on the bus.

(2) Lead riders to play games which teach them something about the Christian faith.

Time for Visitation

We have found that Saturday is the best time to get our work done. At 9:00 A.M. each Saturday we meet for planning, training, promotion, and visitation. It has been evident that this meeting is an important factor in stabilizing and in building the quality of the work. Thirty to forty minutes is spent in a general period followed by brief meetings of bus captains with their workers.

During the general period the report of last Sunday is discussed. Attention is focused on attendance, new riders, the arrival time at Sunday School, the number of hours spent in visitation, the number of persons personally contacted, and the number making professions of faith. Crews with outstanding reports are asked to share what methods were used.

After the report has been discussed time is then spent in planning and coordinating the work. Goals are set for growth and for high attendance days. Parents days are planned from time to time. Plans for special seasons such as Christmas are considered. Plans for new routes or adjustments in routes are worked out. Matters needing coordination between the Sunday School or the worship services are discussed.

Some time is also spent each week in training to improve the quality of our work. Subjects discussed include: dealing with indifferent parents, how to make the Saturday morning visits, how to witness to the lost, how to locate and enlist new riders, how to handle discipline problems, values of the bus ministry, how to deal with problem children, how to deal with poverty needs, how to make the best use of riding time on the buses, how to organize the bus route. We also have tape-recorded training sessions and make them available for new workers to use at home.

Record books are updated and new riders are plotted on a bus map which is maintained.

In addition to all of the above the Saturday meeting is planned to give inspiration. This may be done in a closing prayer or by sharing testimonies, or by a brief devotional thought.

The second part of the Saturday morning meeting is used by bus captains to plan with their outreach visitors. During the last fifteen minutes the bus crews quickly make plans for visitation for the day. New families who may have been turned in by Sunday School workers or have been found on the newcomer list are assigned. Some discussion is given to canvassing new blocks in order to expand the route. Primarily, however, plans are made to see that every family on the route is visited. Some time is also spent updating the church bus records. New families are also plotted on a large map which shows the location of every home being reached. Special activities, such as picnics, trips to the zoo, or parents' days, are planned. In summary, this time is used by captains and crews to work out the detailed plans of their routes. Most activities are planned and carried out separately by individual routes. Occasionally, however, all buses enter into promotional emphases together.

Great effort is taken to see that this meeting concludes by 10:00 A.M., so that no time is lost from visitation. Visitation is normally completed by 1:00 P.M. However, on days when a special emphasis is planned some workers spend the entire day in visitation. Most routes can be built and maintained with a captain and a crew of two or three workers visiting two or three hours each Saturday.

It is important that personal contacts be made each week. Even during Christmas holidays our workers continued to visit. When asked for suggestions as to what should be done on special holidays, it was overwhelmingly agreed that the Saturday meeting should be continued. The group meets at 10:00 A.M. for prayer and a brief meeting. Every bus has been represented and most riders were visited on Christmas and New Years weekends. Bus attendance actually increased during this season while the Sunday School experienced a general drop in attendance. If all of the Sunday School could be mobilized to continue to visit during the holidays, the attendance drop could possibly be avoided.

The following page is a bus report which is published on our midweek Sunday School promotion sheet and is used for the Saturday bus workers meeting. This particular report is the one of the last Sunday of our first year.

The Sunday Morning Schedule

On Sunday morning all workers and the buses arrive at the church at 8:30. The schedule for the morning is as follows:

8:30 A.M.—Buses and workers arrive at church

8:50–9:00 A.M.—Pick up first rider

9:25 A.M.—Buses return to church for Sunday School

10:50 A.M.—Children's worship and preschool extended service begin

11:30 A.M.—Load riders and return home

12:10 P.M.—Buses return to the church for adults and youth who attend the main worship service.

12:45 P.M.—Workers return to the church and depart for home

The schedule listed above is generally followed. Our plan is to get to the first home around 9:00 A.M. or slightly earlier in order to return to the church by 9:25 or 9:30 A.M. The time a bus begins to pick up passengers varies slightly from bus to bus depending upon the length of the route and the number of riders who are to be picked up. It takes more time, of course, if there are more homes on a route. Buses are often late, but this varies according to the number of passengers who

79 Bus Ministry

BUS REPORT SHEET

April 25

Bus Captain	Bus #	Time Arrived	Pro of Faith	Attd. Riders+Workers-Total	New Riders	Workers Present	Hrs. Vist.	Per. Cont.
Smith	1	9:25		32 + 5 = 37	6	2	5½	79
Oates	2	9:40		45 + 7 = 52	2	4	5	62
Miller	3	9:36		27 + 5 = 32	2	4	3½	51
King	4A	9:25		27 + 4 = 31	0	0	1½	31
	4B	9:45		36 + 4 = 40	3		3	52
Gutenberg	5A	9:40		39 + 4 = 43	4	1	4½	105
	5B	9:35		32 + 5 = 37				
Ross	6	9:40		19 + 6 = 25		1	4	81
Nelson	7	9:25		66 + 6 = 72	7	3	7	60
Thorpe	8	9:45		27 + 5 = 32	6	3	6½	100
Totals				350+51 = 401	30	18	40½	621

ride on a given Sunday or if problems arise, such as waiting on a train or for other traffic.

Children's Worship Services

Following the Sunday School hour special worship services are provided for boys and girls sixth grade and younger. These services became necessary when our buses began to reach eighty to ninety in attendance. Prior to this time Sunday School workers were asked to sit with children during the morning worship service if they were not accompanied by their parents. Many children who ride the buses have little or no background in religious education or Christian worship. The services are suited to the needs of the different age groups.

At first one service was provided for all age groups first through sixth grades. The attendance increased, however, so quickly that this service had to be divided into two services, one for first, second, and third grade children and another for fourth, fifth, and sixth graders. These services have proven to be meaningful experiences for these ages and has eliminated some distractions in the main worship services.

When we first began the children's worship service, it began around 10:50 A.M. and concluded at 12:00 noon to coincide with the main worship service. This proved to present a problem since the buses were unable to depart until all riders were dismissed from the main worship service. Discipline problems would sometime arise while the younger riders waited. It was later decided that the younger services would be dismissed at 11:30 A.M. and the children would be taken home. The bus returns to the church shortly after 12:00 noon for youth and adults. Younger children whose parents attend the main worship service get on their bus at 11:30 A.M. and stay with the bus crew until parents are out of the main service around noon. The family then rides home together.

Extended service for preschoolers also had to be enlarged. Our church for a number of years has provided an extended service for four- and five-year-olds. With the coming of the buses new approaches had to be considered. The number of workers needed has more than doubled. Now following the Sunday School hour, the following routine has been established: the boys and girls are taken to the rest room, have a rest period, then go to "Little Big Church" for a brief worship experience.

This worship period might be described as a glorified group time. The boys and girls sing songs, take the offering, have prayer, and then hear a Bible story. The stories used come from group time materials found in Sunday School, church training, and World Friends publications. Songs are chosen to go along with the story. At the present time we have three such services which average about thirty-five children each in attendance.

This type of service grew out of the experience of our workers. The volunteers who previously served in extended services worked under the guidance of one of our Sunday School teachers who did most of the planning. Efforts to involve volunteers in training experiences and in planning for these important minutes with our boys and girls normally had produced little results. Volunteers often expressed the conviction that they didn't feel they did anything beyond "keeping the boys and girls." However, with the use of the routine discussed above, this attitude has changed. These inexperienced workers worship along with the children and feel that they are helping accomplish meaningful worship and learning experiences. We feel that this is important, and experience is proving that workers are much more willing to volunteer their help.

In addition to the feelings of the workers it is our opinion that these experiences are, of course, valuable to the children in preparing them for attending the main worship service later on. As has been mentioned, songs and stories are chosen suited to the age group. The main difference in these services and group time is the size of the group and the arrangement of chairs into rows. Small benches are used in one service.

A few three-year-old preschoolers who ride on the buses are provided for in the extended service. They remain with the rest of their age group until time for the buses to leave. Later we hope to separate these so that any disruption caused by the bus children leaving early can be avoided.

New Member Orientation

From the beginning a good number of the riders have continued to make their professions of faith. Some make decisions on Sunday night while others come during the service for fourth, fifth, and sixth grades. (All persons must present themselves in one of the main worship services). Since transportation is not provided on Sunday night, new member orientation is conducted following Sunday School. Riders who attend this training program, however, do not get to attend the worship service. Some consideration has been given to having this study after the children's worship service at 11:30 A.M. No doubt, adjustments will be made in the days ahead to make the best use of the available time.

Sunday Morning Procedure on the Buses

As has been mentioned, bus workers and the city transit buses arrive at approximately 8:30 A.M. Drivers and bus captains sign in on a roster like the one on page 83.

The bus captain and crew pick up their bus signs, materials, and records (usually maintained by the captain) and board their bus. One sign is placed in the front window of the bus, another is placed near the front door, and a sign indicating the number of the bus is attached to a side window, all clearly visible. A small plastic bag with stick-on name tags, a hand stamp which corresponds to the bus number, and a stamp pad is provided for each bus.

With these things in hand the bus makes its way to the first home. *Each child is picked up at his front door.* The bus pulls up, the driver blows his horn, if necessary, waits for children to board, and drives

83 Bus Ministry

Run	DRIVERS Name	Equipment #	CAPTAIN Name	Bus Route #
1				
2				
3				
4				
5				
6				
7				
8				
9				
10				

immediately to the next home. As the men visit on Saturday they try to determine who will be riding the next morning. The bus goes only to the homes of those who indicate they will be riding. Of course the captain will go to any home where there is the possibility of picking up passengers. They simply do not go to a home if riders expect to be out of the city or indicate that they definitely will not be riding for other reasons.

As boys and girls get on the bus, the captain checks them present, and another worker stamps the bus number on one of their hands. This helps to insure that the rider will get back to the correct bus following worship. Stick-on name tags are placed on all new riders and all preschool passengers. These name tags include the name, the address of new riders, and the Sunday School department room number. It is designed to help get each person to his correct department.

When six or eight boys and girls are on the bus, someone begins to lead the group in the singing of songs or in playing games. Songs and games are designed to contribute to the enjoyment of those who ride and at the same time are chosen for inspirational and educational value. Song sheets have been prepared.

Usually teenagers are used to lead in singing and in games and this is considered to be a very important part of the bus ministry.

As the bus gets near the church, the captain often calls the group to attention and leads in a prayer. This is done to call for God's blessings for the boys and girls as they attend Bible study and worship. It also serves to set the tone for the experience which will be shared.

When the bus pulls up to the church, Sunday School workers meet them at the door. Each department is responsible for having someone meet the bus each Sunday. Older riders depart from their bus and go directly to their department unless they are new riders. New passengers are classified and escorted to their rooms. Preschoolers are then escorted to their rooms by department representatives. Bus captains and crew members remain on their buses to see that every rider is identified and to insure that good discipline is maintained.

It is the Sunday School workers' responsibility to meet the buses when they arrive at church, get riders to their departments, to the worship services, and back to the buses. Bus crews are responsible for picking the riders up at their homes, getting them to the church and returning them to their homes. This seems to be the most clear-cut division of responsibilities, especially as the number of riders increase.

Returning Home

The captain and his crew return to the bus a few minutes before 11:30 A.M. in order to be present when the first rider loads for the trip back home. This helps insure that good discipline is maintained and that all riders are accounted for. Each rider is then returned to his front door with a friendly good-by from the captain and crew members. Every effort is made to call the riders by name and to express joy that they have been in Bible study worship. We consider this to be of great value. Every effort is made to help each rider feel his importance as an individual and understand that we care for him and love him.

Food and Clothing

Not long after the bus ministry got underway it became quickly evident that many riders needed food and clothing. One Sunday last November a family of six came making their professions of faith. One of our adult directors walked through the receiving line and noted that one of the eleven-year-old girls did not have on shoes. He told his department about the experience on the following Sunday. They responded with more than $175.00 on that day and have since that time continued to buy shoes for all who need them. One family of nine was outfitted with shoes at Christmas time, thanks to this department. One of the department members, a shoe store operator, supplied the shoes at a price below his cost. Only God knows the great joy that has come to our church as members have responded to these human needs.

The ladies of Woman's Missionary Society, along with our church benevolence committee, have set up a clothing closet and a pantry. It has been amazing to see the response of the people as they have brought literally hundreds of items, such as dresses, shirts, trousers, underclothing, shoes, and coats.

When the pantry was set up, the Sunday School challenged its members to bring food. People responded with great sacks of canned goods and staple items with a seeming determination that every need in the entire city would be met. Church members have provided for other needs as well. Several families were found without electrical refrigeration in their homes. These were given or provided in other ways. Beds, chairs, and curtains have been donated.

At Christmas time a list of needy families was compiled and made available for Sunday School departments, classes, and individuals. They responded in various ways to provide gifts, food, clothing, and toys. Their efforts were coordinated by the church receptionist who kept records of who was helping whom. Many families would have nothing at Christmas if our members had not responded. God has shown us once again that opportunities for evangelistic outreach and opportunities for expressing social concern go hand in hand. We at Travis do not see a distinction between the two. We believe that the Christian faith in its normal expression will not only care for the spiritual needs of people but will minister to the total person.

Building the Route with Goals and Special Days

Bus captains and workers respond readily to the use of goals and special days. On each Saturday morning some time is spent reviewing progress toward these goals. Goals are set for an average attendance which the crew wishes to be maintaining by a given day. This gives each crew a sense of direction in their work and a gauge by which to measure their efforts. From time to time goals are set for a high attendance. These special days are usually built around the seasons of the year or in cooperation with Sunday School high attendance days.

Goals are especially useful in the bus ministry. Since the bus workers are primarily dealing with outreach they apparently have a greater recognized need to measure their work than do Sunday School workers. Teachers often measure their accomplishments by the "way the lesson went" or by the way the pupils responded to their teaching. Bus workers and perhaps class outreach leaders are more inclined to measure their work more in terms of attendance. So the use of goals is proving to be of great value in the bus ministry.

Where to Start a Route

As has been mentioned earlier, it seems that routes should be started first at the door steps of the church building. Parents seem more willing to let their children ride if they live near the church. Also, canvassers seem to be more responsive to work nearer the church.

Routes should be continually added spreading out from the church into areas of greatest need. It should not be assumed that a neighborhood or community is reached because other churches are already there. Many churches make no effort to reach out for people. Some do little more than provide a preaching service along with Sunday School for those who happen to come. The bus ministry will challenge other churches to consider seriously the matter of outreach. It certainly is to be understood that churches cannot honor Christ by pulling boys and girls or adults away from one church to another. Let's rejoice in the victories of others who honor Christ and make every effort to encourage the loyalty of members to their own church.

Our bus ministry and increased attendance at Travis Avenue has been a source of inspiration to most all of the churches in Fort Worth. Many have expressed their feeling that since Travis' attendance has increased, their own churches have had an upsurge in enthusiasm and outreach, resulting in higher attendance.

As was mentioned previously, areas which offer the greatest potential for starting bus routes are the heavily populated areas, such as trailer courts, apartments, housing projects, isolated areas, military bases, downtown hotels, and moderate to low income single family houses. In many places such as these the population is transient and most churches are unable to adequately cope with the actual needs presented. Since the bus crews visit every Saturday, newcomers can be discovered almost immediately. Very often parents have moved so many times that they seemingly do not intend to settle down and little effort is made to find a church home.

One family of nine children began riding one of our buses at Vacation Bible School time in June, 1970. Seven months later they had lived in four homes and the children had ridden on four different buses. At the time this is written the family has moved again and cannot be located. Almost every week bus workers share with each other the names of riders who are moving from one route to another.

After fifteen months' experience it seems apparent that the greatest response to the buses comes from areas where (1) transportation is actually needed, (2) income is lower, and (3) the community is transient. One reason for this, no doubt, is the reluctance or inability of many churches to put forth the effort necessary to reach such homes. Most churches apparently have felt that their efforts and resources are better spent on more stable family situations.

Bus Records

The record system used by our church has been developed as we have gone along. We have sought to keep them as simple as possible, and at the same time to maintain the essential information needed to carry out and to evaluate our work.

A bus captain is at liberty to use whatever kind of record he needs. He normally must have records which can be formed into the order of his route. Some captains prefer a family card such as the sample.

These cards are also placed in route order, are put in ring binders, and serve as a record of attendance.

```
                    BUS OUTREACH INFORMATION

    Family Name_____

    Address_____

    Telephone_____

    List those to ride the bus:

    Name_____ Birthdate_____ Grade_____

    Name_____ Birthdate_____ Grade_____

    Name_____ Birthdate_____ Grade_____

    Name_____ Birthdate_____ Grade_____

    Name_____ Birthdate_____ Grade_____
```

89 Bus Ministry

NAME _____ PHONE _____

ADDRESS _____ ZIP _____

GRADE _____ DATE OF BIRTH _____

DATE STARTED TO RIDE _____ MEMBER OF TRAVIS ___ YES ___ NO

SUNDAY SCHOOL DEPARTMENT _____ DATE BAPTIZED _____

	1st SUN	2nd SUN	3rd SUN	4th SUN	5th SUN
AUGUST					
SEPTEMBER					
OCTOBER					
NOVEMBER					
DECEMBER					
JANUARY					
FEBRUARY					

	1st SUN	2nd SUN	3rd SUN	4th SUN	5th SUN
MARCH					
APRIL					
MAY					
JUNE					
JULY					
AUGUST					
SEPTEMBER					

With the help of the bus captains the bus secretary maintains a duplicate bus record book of each route using the above record card. This book is for office use and the attendance is checked on Sunday morning either by the bus captain or by the bus secretary. This book is kept in route order so that in cases of emergency it can be used to run the route. At the Saturday morning meeting, time is provided to update these records. The bus captain is also asked to turn in a report of his route each Sunday. The form used for this purpose is indicated in the sample. This report is turned in to the bus secretary who copies the information onto a summary report sheet. The information reported by the captain shows the results of the work accomplished by his crew. All information shown on the summary sheet is reproduced on the mid-week Sunday School promotion sheet along with the goals set by each crew.

	BUS #_____ ROSTER	Date_____
Name_____	Address_____	Dept._____
Name_____	Address_____	Dept._____
Name_____	Address_____	Dept._____
Name_____	Address_____	Dept._____
Name_____	Address_____	Dept._____
Name_____	Address_____	Dept._____
Name_____	Address_____	Dept._____
Name_____	Address_____	Dept._____
Name_____	Address_____	Dept._____
Name_____	Address_____	Dept._____
Name_____	Address_____	Dept._____
Name_____	Address_____	Dept._____
Name_____	Address_____	Dept._____
Name_____	Address_____	Dept._____
Name_____	Address_____	Dept._____

As each rider is picked up, his name and address is written down. The advantage of this record is that new riders are included along with the regular riders. Also on the return trip the list serves as a route sheet. This form is especially helpful to new captains or on new routes where names and addresses are unfamiliar to the worker.

It should be understood that bus records are completely separate from the Sunday School record system. A rider, of course, must be present in his Sunday School department if he is counted in Sunday School attendance. Sunday School workers do, however, refer to the bus records to get additional information for use in their work with the pupil.

Attitude of Church Members

Very often we are asked, "What do your members think about the bus ministry?" We are quick to answer that our people are thrilled by the opportunity offered through bus outreach. In trying to understand why Travis members have responded so favorably toward the buses we have come to these conclusions. First, we began using the buses one year for Vacation Bible School. Sunday School members canvassed four hundred blocks inviting people to attend. So many children requested transportation that we decided to run two buses even though we had not budgeted for them. This was discussed with our Sunday School directors on the Wednesday night before the school was to begin. One director said he would give $100.00 toward the additional expense, and one by one others offered to pay for one day each until one bus was underwritten.

This spirit has characterized our workers and members from the beginning of the bus ministry. Perhaps one reason for it was the fact that approximately four to six hundred of our people were involved in pre-enrolling the boys and girls both for Vacation Bible School and for the bus ministry. This was not something that a few bus captains did. It was a church-wide effort. As our members had a part in locating persons needing transportation they were also made aware of the need first hand. Christian people will respond to a need when it is understood.

Another factor pleasing to our members has been the evangelistic results of this work. On the day the first route was started one beautiful thirteen-year-old girl came making her profession of faith. During Vacation Bible School in 1970, seventy-six made professions of faith, the majority of these having ridden on the buses. During the first seven months of this current year 290 have been baptized. Again, the majority of these have been reached as a result of the bus ministry. It has been an exciting and thrilling experience for all Travis members.

A third reason for the acceptance of this ministry is the use of city buses. From the beginning we have been concerned about the image of this work. These buses are attractive, air conditioned, and have qualified, uniformed drivers. Our people know that insurance, maintenance, and depreciation are included in the price of the rental fees and they do not worry about the safety of the riders. All of this apparently has a bearing upon the acceptance of the bus outreach.

CHAPTER VI
VACATION BIBLE SCHOOL

Excitement is the word to describe what the people of Travis Avenue have felt as we have seen Vacation Bible School attendance double during the last two years. Prior to that time, we were having a good quality school each year with some unchurched boys and girls attending, but most who came were within our own church family. Workers would come with their cars packed, and they worked hard to see that good learning experiences were planned. We prided ourselves on the smoothness of our school, yet there was a sameness about it year after year.

In 1969 we began to catch the vision that we should make a greater effort to reach our immediate community. Special plans were made to canvass an area ten blocks in each direction from the church buildings. Our Sunday School departments and classes enlisted members and went door to door to canvass four hundred blocks. Over five hundred boys and girls were pre-enrolled for Vacation Bible School. Almost none of these had ever been inside our church buildings and most did not attend any other church.

As our people went door-to-door, they would say, "We are having Vacation Bible School for the boys and girls in our community and would like to know if there are children in your home who would like to attend." The response was tremendous. Our neighbors openly expressed their appreciation. Some said, "We don't have children, but we want to commend you on what your church is doing."

No plans had been made to provide transportation, but so many requests were reported that two buses were chartered. On the first day of the school only twenty-one persons rode on the buses, but by the end of the school eighty to one hundred were riding each day. Our people were so pleased that they gladly contributed to pay the extra expense. When the last day of the 1969 Vacation Bible School came, enrollment had reached 954, average attendance 721, and 37 had made professions of faith. This compared to the previous year's enrollment of 728, average attendance of 540, and 18 professions of faith.

The spirit of our workers was the highest ever. They felt that our church was doing what it "ought to be doing." We had experienced a new dimension in outreach.

The Second Year—Spectacular

The next year was truly spectacular. With the knowledge of the blessing of God in 1969 our sights were set higher. Plans were made for the Sunday School to canvass 600 blocks, extra departments were planned, 250 workers were enlisted, and six buses were budgeted.

As canvass packets were turned in, it became apparent that at least ten buses would be needed. Approximately 850 boys and girls were pre-enrolled with over 500 indicating that they needed transportation.

When we approached the first day of Bible school, there was an air of expectancy. Also, there was some anxiety as we wondered how we would be able to pick up three to five hundred boys and girls by bus, get them to their departments, accomplish a meaningful learning experience, and get them back home. This was a mammoth undertaking with new drivers, new bus workers, and for the most part, new Vacation Bible School teachers and directors. On that first day 1,044 attended with approximately 350 riding on our ten chartered buses. Bus routes were adjusted and two new buses were added on the second day—481 riders came plus 36 workers. Our total attendance in Vacation Bible School reached over 1,100. When the 1970 school was over, 1,448 had been enrolled, an average of 1,093 attended for the eight days, and 76 had made professions of faith.

There was an undescribable sense of excitement, thanksgiving, and satisfaction on the part of all the workers. They seemed so grateful that God had used them in touching the lives of literally hundreds of unchurched homes.

One ten-year-old girl who came by bus made her profession of faith during one of the commitment services. She and both her parents came presenting themselves as candidates for baptism at the close of the Bible School on parents' night. One boy came with his father and both requested baptism. Later his mother professed Christ; now all the family is Christian. This happened over and over again. Workers won pupils; pupils won parents or, in some cases, workers won parents. Names of unenlisted parents and entire families were given to our Sunday School teachers and Sunday by Sunday these people are being won to Christ.

Pre-Enrolment Plan

Let's discuss briefly how the pre-enrolment plan is carried out in our church. Blocks are assigned to individuals who go door to door locating boys and girls who would like to attend Vacation Bible School. Canvassers receive packets with a supply of hand bills and pre-enrolment cards.

The handbill varies each year but is designed to provide parents and children with information about the school. It is also used as an

PRE-ENROLLMENT

SPECIAL INSTRUCTIONS:

1. Knock on each door in the block indicated below and do the following:
   (a) <u>Say</u>: We are having Vacation Bible School at Travis Avenue Baptist Church June 21-27 and we are inviting boys and girls 3 to 14 years of age to attend.
   (b) <u>Ask</u>: Do you have boys and girls this age in your home?
   (c) <u>If they do</u>: Could we enroll them for Vacation Bible School? Fill out a card on each family with each child's name, address, date of birth and grade.
   (d) <u>Give a copy</u> of the Clown for each child. Say: "A small prize will be given to those who turn it in for the Picture Coloring Contest on the first or second day of Vacation Bible School.
   (e) <u>If no one is home</u> - leave a copy of the Clown on the door or mail box.
   (f) <u>If no children live in the home</u>, say: "Thank you and Good-bye.

2. <u>Bus Transportation</u>:
   (a) Ask: "Do the children need a ride to Vacation Bible School?" (Check card)
   (b) Ask: "Would you like for the children to ride the bus to Sunday School and worship each Sunday?" (Check card)

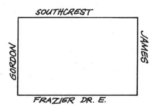

Canvasser's Name_____Dept._____
( ) This is a good block
( ) Do not canvass this block in the future because:_____
_____

Vacation Bible School

```
             VACATION BIBLE SCHOOL NEIGHBORHOOD PRE-ENROLLMENT
    Family Name_____Phone_____

    Address_____

    List those to attend:

        Name_____Birthdate_____Grade_____

        Name_____Birthdate_____Grade_____

        Name_____Birthdate_____Grade_____

        Name_____Birthdate_____Grade_____

        Name_____Birthdate_____Grade_____

    Bus Transportation Needed (✓):

        ( ) V.B.S.      ( ) Sunday School and Worship
```

attraction to the children. Each year a picture is printed on it for a "Picture Coloring Contest." Instructions tell the children to color the picture and bring it with them to Vacation Bible School. Each child who colors his picture and turns it in, receives a balloon when he comes to Bible School.

The pre-enrolment is carried out through the Sunday School. Adult departments receive twenty-five to forty blocks to canvass, depending upon the number of classes and their average attendance. Youth and younger departments receive one block assignment for each church-elected worker enrolled.

On Sunday two weeks before Vacation Bible School begins, lunch is provided for canvassers at the church. After the meal a brief time is spent in demonstrating how to canvass a block. Canvassers are urged to complete their work and turn in their completed packets on that afternoon.

The assignment envelope has the block assignment diagrammed in a space provided and includes brief instructions.

The pre-enrolment card is used to get only the essential information needed.

When cards are completed by canvassers, they are duplicated, assigned for follow-up prior to the school, and are used in setting up bus routes. Children are not actually enrolled in Vacation Bible School until they attend. Following the school all families are placed in the prospect file unless it is determined that they actually attend another church.

Providing Transportation

As boys and girls are pre-enrolled, they are asked if they need transportation. If so, their pre-enrolment card is marked and their homes are later plotted on a map. One bus route is then planned for each thirty houses.

Bus crews use the pre-enrolment cards to work out the best route for their bus to take. Cards are placed in order of the stops to be made. The first home where children are to be picked up is placed first in the stack, the second home, second, and so on. The crew then drives through their route in a car to make sure that a bus can travel over it. Adjustments, of course, must be made as new riders begin to ride day after day.

Usually routes are organized on the two Sundays preceding Vacation Bible School. On Sunday, eight days before the school, all workers meet for lunch, for instructions, and to form their tentative routes. On the next Sunday they receive additional cards of pre-enrolled children which have come in late. These are worked into their routes. Again, a review of the instructions are given, everything is set in order for the first day of school, and crews drive through their routes for final adjustments.

Sunday bus crews (already established and functioning) work their own routes, when possible. If this is not possible, they do all they can to assist the new crews to set up the routes. By working together new crews can benefit from the experienced workers, and the regular crews will be in a better position to follow up on new families after Vacation Bible School. Every effort is made to expand the bus ministry immediately after Vacation Bible School.

Plan for Parking, Off-loading, and Reloading Buses

One of our parking lots is roped off for the buses. This proves to be of great value in controlling the buses and in getting the children to and from their classrooms. The following diagram shows how the lot is used:

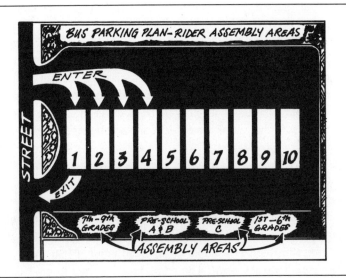

Buses are assigned a definite spot for parking. By having an established parking space for each bus, all drivers, workers, and children benefit. When a bus comes each morning, it is parked in its own designated space. The crew gets on, makes its run, and the bus returns to its designated place to unload. The bus then remains in this parking place to reload when school is out at noon.

You will note in the diagram above that each age division has a designated collection point on the parking lot. Each Vacation Bible School department provides representatives to meet the buses as they arrive. Workers stand behind the age division sign with their own department sign. Usually only one or two buses arrive at the same time. This avoids confusion. Captains are instructed to keep the bus door closed until one of the general officers arrives to help disperse the children. The captain then asks riders to unload in the following order: seventh, eighth, ninth graders first; fourth, fifth, and sixth graders next; first, second, and third graders next and preschoolers last. As they get off the bus, they are directed to the collection point of their age division. Here department workers meet them and take them immediately to their departments. By having the preschoolers last, the unloading goes much faster. Younger children need more assistance in getting out of the bus and to their collection point.

When the school concludes, the department workers are responsible for seeing that each boy and girl gets back to the right bus. Captains check to be sure that all of their riders are accounted for before leaving for the return trip home.

The details for how the boys and girls are identified, taken to the right department, and returned to the correct bus is described in the chapter entitled "Outreach Through Bus Ministry." In brief, however, each child's hand is stamped as he gets on the bus with a number corresponding to the number of his bus. Also, a stick-on name tag is placed on each rider. His name, department name, department room number are all written on it. The name tags are used to get riders to their departments and the stamp is used to get riders back to their proper bus.

Name tags are prepared each afternoon so that a new one is ready each morning for each rider. Bus captains are instructed to leave their route books in the office after they have returned the children home.

Secretaries then make up name tags for each child. Tags are clipped to the family cards. Some children manage to wear their name tags two or three days while others need a new one every morning. A new one is always ready if it is needed.

Making the Most of Parents' Night

Parents' night can be an extremely effective and useful event. We have come to the conviction that it has three primary purposes. It is to be used to interpret what has happened in Vacation Bible School. It is also a time to present an evangelistic message to both the parents and to the children. Then time should be provided for parents to visit in the departments of their children. The program will vary perhaps from year to year but generally speaking, most churches will have the boys and girls seated in the auditorium by departments and by age division. Parents and children participate in pledges to the flags and to the Bible. A brief time is given to recognizing the workers and giving a statistical report. This is followed by an evangelistic message and an invitation. On parents' night of 1970 at our church fifty-five persons made professions of faith including three parents. After this service the children marched to their departments and waited to greet their parents as they came for open house. Refreshments were served and parents were encouraged to visit in their child's classroom. Workers used this time to explain in more detail what the boys and girls had been learning and doing during the school.

No great emphasis was given to handcrafts. The parents were able to see something of the activities or projects the boys and girls had been involved in during the school. In younger departments things made on the last day of school were left intact for the parents to see.

Buses, of course, ran their routes just as they had each day.

Follow-up for Sunday School

Before Vacation Bible School was over efforts were made to identify each prospect. It was discovered, as has already been mentioned, that the vast majority of those attending the school were not enrolled in any Sunday School or church in Fort Worth. Children's Sunday School departments were asked to visit in the homes to determine the ages of the parents. Since there were so many visits to be made, adult departments were also asked to help.

The purpose of the visit was to determine if the families were prospects. If they did not attend another church regularly, full information was sought on each member of the family so that they could be assigned to a Sunday School department.

In the days following the school several hundred have been reached. Vacation Bible School continues to be an increasingly useful tool for evangelistic outreach. One of the greatest tragedies in most churches is the failure to follow up after Vacation Bible School.

CHAPTER VII
FULL USE OF REVIVALS

A few years back, for two years, our church had only one revival each year which was held in the spring. In the fall, however, we had a week of visitation which we called a visitation revival. The overall result was that less people were baptized in these years than in years when two revivals were held. We learned that there is still great value in an evangelistic emphasis which takes place in a special week of revival services. Church leaders and members seem to rally to revival challenge and seem to find greater opportunity to visit and do personal witnessing during a season of revival services. Special activities planned during the week of revival give members a focal point, and they may invite friends and prospects they have come to know. It is also true that the pastor and the staff better concentrate their efforts through such weeks and find that their efforts can result in an evangelistic harvest.

In the last two years we have returned to the practice of having two major revivals each year. Greater effort has been put into each campaign. More advertising has been used and more activities have been scheduled throughout the week of revival services. And yet little or no promotion is used in the actual revival services themselves. We have not used the "pack the pew" idea and other such approaches which call for recognitions within the services. Every effort has been made to keep each service limited entirely to singing, to welcoming of guests, and to preaching and giving the evangelistic appeal.

Planning the Revival

It is important to get the calendar dates for the revival set up early. Revivals should be put on the calendar and personnel secured at least one year ahead, and, if possible, two or three years ahead. This will enable the church to get qualified persons they feel are needed.

As time nears for the revival, a more detailed calendar of activities should be prepared. This should include preparation meetings, as well as activities to be conducted during the week of revival, and all follow-through activities.

Activities before the revival include witnessing training. A personal evangelism institute might begin on a Sunday night during the church training hour, continue with a message during the worship hour, and then be carried over for one, two or three nights as necessary. These training sessions help to build conviction about the need for witnessing and should give information as well as practical experience in doing witnessing. Training sessions without practical experience usually proves to be of little help in getting members to do personal witnessing.

Another approach which has been helpful is a series of sessions on personal witnessing taught during the Wednesday prayer meeting hour in the weeks leading up to a revival. Training courses may also be held on Sunday night during the church training program. Sunday morning assembly times can be used for marking New Testaments, assigning prospects, and so forth.

Also during the days leading up to the revival every effort should be made to block out certain days for revival visitation. Prospect assignments need to be made two to three weeks prior to the first Sunday of the revival in order to give people ample time to visit their prospects one or two times before the meetings begin. Often every prospect in our file is assigned through the mail with a letter giving instructions for the visits to be made. Our members and our prospects are kept in our addressing plate file, and efforts are made to assign prospects to members who live in the same zip code zone within the city. This, of course, saves members time since they will be visiting persons located near their own houses. Members are asked to visit their prospect two times prior to the revival services. On the second visit they are asked to invite them to be their guest at a prospect supper during the revival. Brochures are left in each home and an attempt is made to lead the person to make a definite decision about what services he will attend.

In addition to the general prospect assignment made to all church members, Sunday School members, fourth grade and older who are not church members, are assigned as prospects for evangelism. These are assigned to their classes since teachers usually have the greatest knowledge and influence with their own members. Some Sunday School members who are not church members are also given to church staff and to the revival team for visitation throughout the week of revival services.

Additional assignments are also made to members of the staff. Each staff member is asked to visit a number of hours each day throughout the week of revival. They are assigned some of the key prospects and will make efforts to enlist prospects for prospect suppers and to get the prospects into the services of the revival. More will be said about the prospect suppers later.

Leading up to the revival, prayer partner sign-up cards may be distributed throughout the Sunday School. These cards are used by the department directors and teachers. Usually class members are asked to select a prayer partner within the class. The class outreach leader may divide the class into groups of twos for prayer. Prayer partners are asked to meet to pray daily, if possible. If it is not possible to meet in person, they are to visit by telephone and to have prayer right over the telephone with each other.

Prospect Suppers

During the week of revival services prospect suppers are set up for age groups. These usually begin at 6:30 P.M. or about an hour before services. In a recent revival the following schedule was used:

Monday—4th, 5th, and 6th grade hot dog supper

Tuesday—Family guest (prospect) supper

Wednesday—10th, 11th, and 12th grade youth

Thursday—7th, 8th and 9th, grade youth

Friday—Family guest (prospect) supper

These suppers are usually served at no charge for prospects or for members who bring prospects. The younger age groups, especially the fourth, fifth, and sixth grades, will be served hot dogs or hamburgers, while the junior high group will normally be served hamburgers or a full meal. Older youth and adult groups are served ham, roast beef, or fried chicken.

Usually meals are served buffet style. At the close of each meal the pastor is called on to give a welcome and to introduce the revival team. At times the plan of salvation is explained but usually no invitation is given. Information is shared about the church program. After the meal, adult groups are very often given a guided tour of the church facilities. Then the group is escorted to the sanctuary to await the beginning of the service.

The supper offers an opportunity to express the warmth of the congregation and, of course, to get the people out for the revival services. Experience has shown that many who come to the suppers join the church. Some join on the night of the supper and others through the next few weeks. Revival activities such as these make it possible for Sunday School workers of every age group, to focus in on their department members. All age groups are systematically sought for any decisions that need to be made.

Revival Publicity

Of course there are numerous ways to advertise a revival. The basic ways that are used by our church are listed below:

1. *Brochure.*—A brochure is usually prepared which includes pictures of the revival team and the schedule of revival services. This brochure is cut in such a way that it will fit into an envelope for mailing and can be used as a poster in Sunday School departments, store fronts, etc.

2. *Mailouts to members.*—As was discussed earlier, letters are sent to all church members with a brochure and a prospect assignment. Members are asked to give the brochure to the prospect when they visit. It serves a dual purpose of providing members with information about the revival and gives them a direct opportunity to become involved in reaching someone for the revival.

3. *Mailout to prospects.*—Each time a revival is held prospects are sent a brochure. As has been mentioned, all prospect family units are kept in our address file and, therefore, we take this opportunity to have a contact with each home.

4. *Posters.*—Very often our brochure makes an attractive poster. These posters are placed in store windows and in places of business operated by our members. At times special large posters are made with glossy print pictures which can be set up as a display in prominent places. Some local banks have been willing to have the display set in their downtown lobbies. Some members who manage or own stores or restaurants have allowed us to place large attractive posters on easels in a prominent place where customers can view them.

5. *Paid advertisements.*—The use of the local newspaper and radio is one of the best ways to get the message out to a large cross section of the population. Usually newspaper ads are run the Thursday or Friday prior to the revival. Then on Saturday a large ad is

used showing the personalities and giving directions to the church. Throughout the week of services additional smaller ads are placed in both morning and evening papers. On Saturday of the closing weekend a major ad is again run inviting people to the closing services.

Radio spots have been used effectively. Ten-second, thirty-second, and one-minute spots are used beginning on Thursday before the revival and then throughout the week of the revival, concluding on Saturday.

Television spots, of course, are very desirable, but have only recently become available in Fort Worth.

6. *Free advertising.*—Very often free newspaper, radio, and television advertising can be secured. Care should be made to write up newspaper articles and to get them in approximately one week before they are to be used. Announcements should be prepared for radio and television and mailed to the community service broadcasts of every radio and television station in the entire area. Many stations will make the announcement preceding both weekends if the information is received in time.

7. *Church paper.*—The church newspaper, of course, is a basic source for advertising the revival. An article might appear in the paper when personnel is first secured, even a year or six months ahead of time. During the six weeks or so immediately preceding the revival a series of articles should be placed in the church paper. One week, the biographical data about the evangelist, along with a picture can be used. Another week the musician can be introduced. Various activities which will be taking place prior to and during the revival, such as an evangelism institute or soul winning class gives opportunity to mention the dates of the revival. On the weekend immediately preceding the revival a major display all across the front page is helpful. The personalities, the time schedule, and special events which will be taking place each night during the week should be outlined.

8. *The Sunday Bulletin.*—The Sunday bulletin or order of service can be used most effectively to help advertise the revival. Beginning

a month or so before the revival, basic information might be placed on the back of the bulletin enclosed in a small box. Reference, of course, could be made to this during the announcement period in the service. Two weeks, or one week, prior to the first service pictures of the evangelist and the schedule of the meeting might be placed on the front cover of the bulletin. Then, of course, on the beginning Sunday of the revival this might be used again. Care should be taken to see that this be prepared in good taste so that it will contribute to the worship services in which the bulletin is to be used.

9. *Songbook covers.*—Songbook covers can be prepared giving basic information about the revival and possibly pictures of the evangelist or of the revival team. These can be used in Sunday School departments and in the sanctuary. If they are used in the sanctuary it will not be necessary to put the pictures on the front of the Sunday bulletin as mentioned above.

10. *Announcements in the Sunday School departments.*—Sunday School directors and outreach leaders play an important role in interpreting the revival to the members of the Sunday School departments. Leading up to the revival, announcements should be made about the personalities, the schedule, and the special events. And, of course, songbook covers, if used in the departments, can be referred to in the announcements.

11. *Handbills.*—A handbill or brochure canvass can be made by youth. Very often our young people are involved in taking specially prepared handbills or brochures and going door to door in certain areas of the city.

12. *Invite outside groups.*—It is often helpful for the pastor to send a letter to all pastors of other Baptist churches in the city to inform them about the services. This serves to give opportunity for other churches to participate in the revival and also helps to build attendance for the meeting. Prospects, football teams, or other youth groups may be invited to a guest supper or to special services where an emphasis will be placed upon youth.

In summary, every effort should be made to get the word out to everyone involved. No matter how strategic the meeting is or how much preparation has gone into it the result is certain to be limited unless the word gets out to the people who need to attend.

Revival Counselors

In the last year or so an effort has been made to enlist counselors to be used in our revival services. They are carefully selected by the pastor or church staff members. Usually our new member orientation counselors are included in the group along with Sunday School teachers and others who are capable of doing personal work. A number of young people, high school and college age, are included in the group so that they are available to counsel other young people their own ages. Counselors are enlisted a few weeks before the revival and at least one instruction period is held prior to the services. A good time for this session is on Sunday morning at 9 A.M. or just prior to the Sunday School hour. An instruction sheet is passed out and explained. Counselors are given tips on how to dress, how to conduct themselves in a counseling session, how they will be used in the services during the invitation and following the close of the service. They receive help on counseling and are prepared to be used in a number of ways. They may be assigned to come forward on a certain verse of the song during the invitation hymn which means there will be people coming throughout the invitation, some on the first verse, some on the second, some on the third and fourth verses, etc. They stand in a place where they can see the staff members who are receiving people as they come forward. When a person comes forward, a staff member greets them, counsels briefly with them, and then calls for a counselor. The counselor then helps the person fill in the decision card and to answer any question he may have. Following the service those who have come forward are presented to the congregation and immediately following are dismissed to go with their counselor to the counseling room.

In the counseling room materials concerning the new member orientation program of the church are passed out. Information is given about the content of the course and the necessity for each person to attend. Materials are given, such as the church calendar and other information considered to be helpful in getting the new member to become active in the Bible teaching, worship and training program of the church. Those who have come by profession of faith are given instructions about baptism. After a closing prayer, counselors are available for any further question or discussion.

The time taken for this is kept to a minimum. Usually less than fifteen minutes is needed from the time the group leaves the sanctuary and goes to the counseling room. Of course those who have particular problems remain with their counselor as long as necessary after the group is dismissed.

Follow Up

As can be seen above, follow up begins immediately at the close of each service. New member orientation is carried out on Sunday evening during the church training program. Sessions are taught in rotation so that a new member may begin on any night. However, on the first night a new member attends, he is placed with a counselor and is asked to give his conversion experience and to answer a few questions concerning his experience as a Christian. Adults are questioned about previous service in the church, such as Sunday School teaching. New Christians receive further counseling concerning the meaning of the conversion experience and concerning the importance and the meaning of baptism.

All new members are assigned to a Sunday School department for visitation immediately following the revival and every effort is made to see that they are enlisted for regular Bible study and worship. Deacons are assigned to visit in the homes of all new members to encourage them to become active in the church program. Those who have come for baptism are visited or are telephoned by a church staff member to arrange for his baptism. Letters are also sent out to all new members urging them to attend Sunday School and giving them the room number of their department. In the last two years we have had high attendance day on Sunday, one week following the closing service of the revival. This, of course, helps to get new members to attend a full day of Bible study, worship, and training on the Sunday immediately following his decision. This has proven useful in continuing the revival through an additional week. During our last revival we had more than thirty additions on the Sunday following the revival.

Youth and Special Personalities

During the spring of 1971 our pastor preached our revival, our music director led the singing, and special attractive personalities were invited to give their Christian testimony each night during the week. Personalities chosen were known to be people outside the church membership and outside of Christian circles. They included Coach Tom Landry of the Dallas Cowboys; Bob Harrington, chaplain of Bourbon Street; Roger Staubach, quarterback for the Dallas Cowboys; Debbie Patton, Miss Teenage America, 1970; Terry Bradshaw, quarterback for the Pittsburgh Steelers; and Phyllis George, Miss America 1971. Each of these personalities had a certain attraction to young people, as well as to other age groups. They were asked to take about fifteen minutes during the early part of the service to give their personal testimony. Our minister of music planned the service with a great choir but with fewer congregational songs than we would normally have in a revival service. After the testimony was given we had special music and then the pastor preached a message taking about twenty-five minutes. This was all done with great effectiveness and without prolonging the services. Crowds for the revival were the largest we have had and our people entered into the services as never before.

Perhaps the greatest single value of the use of the personalities was the interest shown through the local news media and people outside of church circles. One of the local newspapers, *The Fort Worth Press,* made it front page news, citing the personalities and showing pictures of each. This in itself is unusual for Fort Worth papers. A local radio station covered each service and reported it on the ten and eleven o'clock newscast. Both city newspapers and most radio and television stations were more than willing to give free announcements concerning the meeting. Our church got the attention of the city by giving these outstanding personalities a chance to give a witness either in person or through an announcement in the newspaper. They were taking a stand for Christ and were challenging people throughout the city to turn to him.

Revival Visitor Registration

We have found that the use of a special revival visitor registration form is useful. As people enter the church service they receive a single slip of paper, 8½ by 5½ inches in size, entitled "Revival News." Appropriate announcements are printed at the top of the sheet and the bottom half of the sheet is a visitor's registration form. Visitors are asked to fill this in and to drop it into the offering plate when it is passed. We can quickly determine whether the person is a prospect or an active member of another local church. Visitors are asked to indicate how they learned about the services. This information helps in planning future advertising and publicity.

Revival Budget

Expenses of a revival should be anticipated and a budget should be set up. After the budget is planned it is presented to the church finance committee for approval. Each expenditure is itemized, such as advertising, brochures, tracts, copies of *Good News for Modern Man,* child care, postage, other printing expenses, hotel or motel expenses for personnel, and, depending on how the honoraria will be handled, they may also be included in the revival budget.

The finance committee then develops plans for securing the needed funds. Usually a small amount is placed in the church budget, but most of the expenses for revival are raised through a special revival offering. The finance committee may send letters to each family in the church membership, along with a special revival expense envelope. This letter is usually sent out during the week immediately preceding the beginning of revival services. Approximately fifty to seventy-five percent of the money needed is given on the first Sunday of the revival. Offerings are taken through the early part of the week to complete the expense offering, and if a love offering is taken it is usually received beginning on Thursday night and in each service until the revival is over.

CHAPTER VIII
TRAINING WITH A PURPOSE

As a result of the studies made by our church we began to take a good hard look at every activity in which we were engaged. One thing that was most obvious was that we had three organizations which were devoted to training or mission education. In an effort to simplify, correlate, and improve our program we decided to combine all of our training groups. The music program might be considered a training program also, but the very nature of choir rehearsal and its content makes it more difficult to be considered along with other training groups.

It was noted that our mission groups for preschoolers, children, and youth continually struggle to maintain quality work and an adequate corps of leaders. We had come to the conviction that missions training was of great importance. Yet some of the missions education groups were more lacking than any part of the training program. This was not due to the lack of effort of our missions leaders but we felt that it was due largely to the time these groups met for their work. After long discussion and serious thought it was decided that the Sunday night training program and the missions program for all age groups would be combined into a single training program.

Another area of missions training which suffered almost entirely from the lack of interest was that of the Brotherhood. Our men had customarily had a monthly meeting, usually with supper and a speaker. Efforts would be made at each meeting by the mission action leader to involve the men in mission action projects. The great problem seemed to be that most of those who attended were deacons, Sunday School department directors and teachers, training leaders, staff members and others who were already carrying heavy work loads in the church. It was felt that training sessions for mission activities should be held on Sunday night during the church training hour, and that Sunday school classes should be asked to undertake various mission activities. The Sunday School classes have men in their groups who are not already overly involved in other church responsibilities and could as a unit or as individuals find purpose and meaning in undertaking mission action projects. A mission action planning group, coordinated through the church Missions Committee suggests class projects of mission needs. Classes in turn choose what action or project they will undertake. If an adult Sunday School class accepted only one or two projects a year the results would be fantastic. It will take time for this approach to be fully implemented in our church, but already classes at Travis Avenue are coming to find greater purpose in meaningful missions activities.

Missions education for men is not optional. The monthly meetings often reached a small percentage of our men and most received absolutely no exposure to missions action or education except through the pulpit ministry. Again it was felt that perhaps the meeting time was one of the greatest problems.

Materials provided in our mission education publications are outstanding and serve as the major source for building our Sunday evening missions training program. The missions action manuals have also proven to be especially useful. More will be said later about courses of study offered.

Need to Train More Purposefully

One of the great needs that our leaders have discovered is that of involving adults in planning their courses of study. Involvement was limited to those faithful persons who attended the regular Sunday night training sessions. Most adults had little or nothing to say about what training they needed or what their interests were. So the idea of a questionnaire was introduced to allow the people themselves to decide what subject interested them.

Let us now mention the matter of grouping adults for the church training. Many courses can best be taught with adults grouped by age, but at times it is of little importance, depending upon the nature of the course content. Adults are now asked to choose the courses they will study. If an adult is interested in more than one course offered during a given period of study, he chooses one now and waits for others to be offered later. Some courses are offered twice during the same year.

Surveys have been conducted to determine what courses interested our adults. From these studies the following observations were made:

1. A keen interest in Bible survey courses was shown. New Testament and Old Testament has received the highest rating each time a poll has been taken. Also of great interest is a study of a book of the Bible and principles of Bible interpretation.

2. Great interest has been shown in practical courses such as Christian parents getting along with their teenagers, Christian family money management, improving personal efficiency, and other studies related to family or personal needs.

3. A willingness to train for a specific leadership task or position is always evident. The teacher as a counselor, learning to witness, how to prepare a Sunday School lesson plan, are examples of courses offered.

4. An interest in training for mission action projects is expressed along with a desire to learn about all areas of missions.

5. And finally, a great interest is shown in courses related to the developmental tasks of the age group. In other words, adults want help with the particular problems they are facing in life whether it be marriage, vocation, rearing of children, or old age.

The purposes of our church training program have grown out of what we have learned in surveys, the response of our people, and our own conviction about the purposes of the church. They are as follows:

1. To meet personal needs of individuals. By this we mean that courses are to be provided which will help individual Christians with personal problems related to their home, their work, and their own personal lives. These studies always get the greatest response of attendance in the Sunday night training program.

2. Our second purpose is to meet the desire for further knowledge of the Bible, of doctrine, of history, and of ethical issues of the Christian faith.

3. A third purpose is to meet the needs of our church program for specific leadership training. Courses are provided to train interpreters in the sign language for a recently established deaf ministry. Conversational Spanish has been offered to provide leaders with enough skill to make effective visits in homes where family members speak Spanish. (This is especially valuable in the state of Texas where a great number of people are of Spanish and Mexican descent.) Tentative plans call for establishing a Spanish-speaking teaching and worship program. When our bus ministry was started, training sessions were offered to train bus workers. Also we have a literacy ministry both for teaching illiterates and for training literacy teachers. Whatever the specific needs of the church are, whether for Sunday School teachers or others mentioned, training will be provided and most of this training is done on Sunday night.

In conclusion, the purposes of our training program are to meet personal needs of individuals, to train members in church membership and Christian development, and to provide leadership training to support the church program.

The Adult Training Program

In the past two years we have learned much that has been helpful in improving our adult training. Experience with leadership training programs have shown us that short courses are usually more successful than longer ones. Our first leadership courses included the Potential Leadership and Training Sunday School Workers materials published by the Sunday School Board. This was set up on Sunday and Wednesday night for a period of six months. Our experience was that by the end of the course only eight to ten persons would graduate out of a beginning class of 25 to 30. Although graduates were well qualified, they were too few in number to meet the needs for leaders in our church. Later the content of both courses were combined into an eleven week course. Obviously some of the material had to be eliminated. The results, however, was that many more workers were provided. Even then, during the last few weeks of the course students would drop out. Based upon this experience and the problem of providing leaders and teachers of the highest quality, we decided upon courses of six to seven weeks in length.

The benefits of such an approach are many. First, all courses can begin at the same time. Although some courses may follow in sequence, one period after another, by having all begin at the same time, the "drop outs" can choose a new course at the beginning of a new six- or seven-week period of study.

Another benefit of the short course approach is that the church training program gets a major emphasis once each six or seven weeks. New members coming into the church are challenged to begin with new member orientation if they did not begin on the first Sunday they joined the church. (New members are asked to attend an eight week program which is rotated so that members may enter the study on any

Sunday night.) All members are challenged to join in for one of the "new" courses beginning "tonight."

If a program leader desires to have a course of study for age group workers or for a missions action project, he may begin and complete his course to coincide with a complete period of study. This makes it possible for all members to have full value of any course that is offered. No one needs to consider himself "idle."

Each course leader turns in an outline showing each session of study. He is to list the sub-topic for each night of the six weeks and is to indicate who the leader or teacher will be. This has proven to be a great asset. It helps to insure good planning and to provide the information needed to interpret the content of the course. A detailed outline is published each six-week period showing what will take place in each course in each session of study. It is then published and distributed in all Sunday School departments with a brief announcement on the first Sunday of each training period. This entire outline is also printed on the back of the Sunday order of service. Often the mention is made of the value of the courses offered at the close of the Sunday morning services.

Using the Questionnaire

Below is listed the first questionnaire used:

INTEREST SURVEY
Church Training Program

September–December 1969

If the following courses of study were offered on Sunday night and if you were to attend, how interested do you feel you would be in each of the following subjects: (check_____)

Note: Most courses will be 6 weeks long.

Very Int.	Some Int.	Little Int.	
____	____	____	Christian Family Money Management
____	____	____	Survey of the Old Testament
____	____	____	Survey of the New Testament
____	____	____	Christian Parents Understanding Teenagers
____	____	____	How to prepare a Sunday School Lesson Plan
____	____	____	Effective use of Audio Visuals
____	____	____	Using the Lecturing Method in Teaching
			Panorama of World Missions and Behold! My Neighbors (Our Texas Baptist River Ministry on the Rio Grande)
____	____	____	Mission Action: Juvenile Rehabilitation
____	____	____	Mission Action: Working with Language Groups
____	____	____	Mission Action: Working with Non-Readers
____	____	____	Mission Action: Prison Rehabilitation
____	____	____	Mission Study: *Sons of Ishmael* (Story of Arabs)
____	____	____	Group Learning Principles
____	____	____	Principles of Bible Interpretation
____	____	____	Basic Leadership Principles
____	____	____	Witnessing to Specific Groups (Catholics, Jews, Mormons, etc.)
____	____	____	Counseling and Ministering to Individual Needs

___ ___ ___ Christian Marriage
___ ___ ___ Christian Family Planning for Retirement & Further Service
___ ___ ___ Christian Families Planning for Insurance, Wills, etc.
___ ___ ___ Christian Family Recreation
___ ___ ___ Baptist History: *The Baptist March in History*

Circle one of the above subjects you prefer above all others.

PART II

Please indicate briefly how you feel your church (Travis or other churches) has helped you or *failed* you in each of the following situations in your life. Give short answers such as: pastor's messages, teachers counseling, Sunday School Lessons, Training Union Programs, church friends, literature, camps or retreats, special studies, or not at all, etc.

1. In choosing your wife or husband: _____

2. In learning to live with your marriage partner: _____

3. In starting a family (planning for children): _____

4. In rearing children: _____

5. In managing a home: _____

6. In getting started in your occupation: _____

7. In taking on civic responsibility: _____

8. In finding a congenial social group or friends: _____

This questionnaire was made up, keeping in mind both materials and leadership available in our church. All topics included in the questionnaire could be offered. Resource materials to be used are found in publications produced by the Sunday School Board or the mission agencies of our Convention. Some resources were drawn from seminary text books or from men or women in the congregation who have qualifications to lead our people in a particular area of study.

The problem of church training had never been the lack of materials. We simply have never planned adequately to use them. Our approach compels us to plan ahead and to enlist teachers with superior qualifications to lead in the learning experiences. Also, as has been mentioned, our adults are involved both in filling out the questionnaire before courses are set up and in selecting the exact course of study they will follow during each six week period.

Listed below is the actual list of courses offered during the first year of our changed approach. You will note that some subjects were offered but not listed on the questionnaire. Also, some subjects appearing on the questionnaire were not offered. The questionnaire is used to find the interest of the people. What was learned here was considered along with the needs of the projected program of the entire church.

Pre-Enrollment for Adult Training Program

Choose what you plan to study by circling the number of *one* course under *each period* of study. You will note that many courses will be offered twice this year.

First Period—September 7–October 12 (6 weeks)
(Choose One)

1. Old Testament Survey: Through the Old Testament in six weeks.
2. How to Prepare a Sunday School Lesson Plan.
3. Panorama of World Missions: Given by persons who have first hand experience of Southern Baptist Missions.
4. Christian Parents Understanding Teenagers.
5. Witnessing to Special Groups (Catholics, Jews, Mormons, etc.)
6. New Member Orientation
7. Single Adult Union (ages 29-up)
8. Married Seminary Union (married-29)
9. Senior Adult Department

Second Period—October 19–November 30 (7 weeks)
(Choose One)

1. New Testament Survey: Through the New Testament in seven weeks.
2. Counseling and Ministering to Individual Needs.
3. Mission Study: From Texas to Teharan (includes *Sons of Ishmael* by Finley Graham)
4. Christian Family Money Management (budget, credit, insurance, retirement, and wills)
5. Christian Marriage
6, 7, 8, 9. Same as under Period One.

Third Period—December 7–28 (4 weeks)

Mission Studies: Foreign, Home, State, and Local Missions will be presented by missionaries on furlough and others who have had first hand experience in these areas of mission work. (Details to be announced.)
6, 7, 8, 9. Same as under Period One.

Fourth Period—January 4–February 8 (6 weeks)
(Choose One)

1. Bible Interpretation: Principles of interpretation, customs of Bible times and geography of Bible lands.
2. Principles of Developing Your Leadership Ability.
3. Missions: Ministry to Juveniles
4. Christian Responsibility: Alcoholism, narcotics, honesty, gambling, obscenity, organized crime.
5. The Christian and His Church in These Changing Times.
6, 7, 8, 9. Same as under Period One.

Fifth Period—February 15–March 22 (6 weeks)
(Choose One)

1. Old Testament Survey: Through the Old Testament in six weeks.
2. How to Prepare a Sunday School Lesson Plan.
3. Home Missions: "Lord Speak Through Me . . ."
4. Christian Family Money Management (budget, credit, insurance, retirement, and wills).
5. Witnessing to Special Groups (Catholics, Jews, Mormons, etc.)
6, 7, 8, 9. Same as under Period One.

Sixth Period—April 5–May 10 (6 weeks)
(Choose One)

1. New Testament Survey: Through the New Testament in six weeks.
2. Baptist Beliefs
3. Mission Action Group Study
4. Great Revivals and Great Evangelists.
5. War and Peace—A Christian's Responsibility.
6, 7, 8, 9. Same as under Period One.

Seventh Period—May 24–June 28 (6 weeks)
(Choose One)

1. Bible Interpretation: Principles of interpretation, customs of Bible times and geography of Bible lands.
2. Martin Luther and the Reformation.
3. Missions: Christ and the City.
4. Christian Parents Understanding Teenagers.
5. Christian Family Recreation (at home, camping, travel, etc.)
6, 7, 8, 9. Same as under Period One.

Eighth Period—July 12–August 23 (7 weeks)
(Choose One)
1. Baptist History
2. Beliefs of Other Denominations
3. Missions: Study of Books by Contemporary Authorities about the World Today.
4. Persons in Crisis (Ministering to the Losers)
5. Abundant Christian Living
6, 7, 8, 9. Same as under Period One.

Signed_____Dept._____

During the second year of the program the following questionnaire was used. It is apparent that too many subjects were included; however, we were prepared to provide resource materials and leadership for all courses listed:

INTEREST SURVEY (PLEASE DO NOT SIGN)
Church Training Program
September 1970–August 1971

If the following courses of study were offered on Sunday night from 5:45 to 6:45 and if you were to attend, how interested do you feel you would be in each of the following subjects: (check ✓)
Note: Most courses will be 6 weeks long.

Very Int.	Some Int.	Little Int.	
1.			Christian Family Money Management
2.			Survey of the Old Testament
3.			Survey of the New Testament
4.			Christian Parents Understanding Teenagers
5.			How to Prepare a Sunday School Lesson Plan
6.			Counseling and Ministering to Individual Needs
7.			Christian Family Recreation
8.			Baptist History: *The Baptist March in History*

My age range is (circle) 18–25 26–30 31–40 41–55 56–65 65–up

9.			Life and Letters of Paul
10.			Matthew
11.			Psalms
12.			Gensis
13.			Revelations
14.			Archaeology and The Bible
15.			Christian View of Science and the Scripture
16.			How to Interpret the Bible
17.			Baptist Beliefs

	Very Int.	Some Int.	Little Int.	
18.	___	___	___	Beliefs of Other Denominations
19.	___	___	___	History of Christianity in America
20.	___	___	___	History of Texas Baptist
21.	___	___	___	Developing Your Leadership Ability

Understanding, Characteristics and Needs

22.	___	___	___	Pre-Schoolers (Birth-5 years)
23.	___	___	___	Children (6–11 years)
24.	___	___	___	Adults (at various ages)
25.	___	___	___	Youth
26.	___	___	___	Increasing Your Personal Efficiency (How to remember names, read faster, etc.)
27.	___	___	___	Constructive Parent-Child Relationship (how to get along with your children.)
28.	___	___	___	Skills for Ministering to Human Needs
29.	___	___	___	Music: Know Your Hymns-Theological and Doctrinal Interpretations
30.	___	___	___	Music: A study of Composers, Authors, and Hymn Stories
31.	___	___	___	Christian Life and Contemporary Times
32.	___	___	___	Christian Responsibility to Mass Media (T.V. & Magazines and "smut")
33.	___	___	___	Christian Confront Communism
34.	___	___	___	Building a Successful Marriage
35.	___	___	___	How to Witness to a Catholic Friend
36.	___	___	___	How to Witness to a Jewish Friend
37.	___	___	___	Bus Ministry: How to fill a bus in 30 days?
38.	___	___	___	Christianity and World Religions
39.	___	___	___	The Making of a Missionary: From Decision, through preparation, to touching lives

129 Training with a Purpose

	Very Int.	Some Int.	Little Int.	
40.	_____	_____	_____	Baptist Work in South America—Who (culture), What, When, (history) Where, and How (hospitals, schools, etc.)
41.	_____	_____	_____	Baptist Work in Africa—Who (culture), What, When, (history), Where, and How (hospitals, schools, etc.)
42.	_____	_____	_____	Baptist Work in Fort Worth
43.	_____	_____	_____	History of Christian Missions
44.	_____	_____	_____	The New China and Baptist Work
45.	_____	_____	_____	Baptist Work in Asia: Who, etc.—
46.	_____	_____	_____	Baptist Work in Europe: Who, etc.—
47.	_____	_____	_____	Baptist Work in Bible Lands: Who, etc.—
48.	_____	_____	_____	Baptist Work in the U. S. A.: Who, etc.—
49.	_____	_____	_____	Baptist Work in Texas: Who, etc.—

Christians Ministering to:

	Very Int.	Some Int.	Little Int.	
50.	_____	_____	_____	The Aging
51.	_____	_____	_____	Agricultural Migrants
52.	_____	_____	_____	Alcoholics
53.	_____	_____	_____	Baptist Centers and Other Mission Institutions
54.	_____	_____	_____	Economically Disadvantaged
55.	_____	_____	_____	Headliners
56.	_____	_____	_____	Internationals
57.	_____	_____	_____	Juvenile Rehabilitation
58.	_____	_____	_____	Language Groups
59.	_____	_____	_____	The Military
60.	_____	_____	_____	Nonreader
61.	_____	_____	_____	Physically Handicapped
62.	_____	_____	_____	Resort Areas
63.	_____	_____	_____	The Sick
64.	_____	_____	_____	Unwed Mothers

	Very Int.	Some Int.	Little Int.	
65.	_____	_____	_____	Jails and Correctional Institutes
66.	_____	_____	_____	Drug Abusers
67.	_____	_____	_____	The World Today as seen by Contemporary Authors
68.	_____	_____	_____	This Christian and His Church in These Changing Times
69.	_____	_____	_____	The Ministry of the Deacon
70.	_____	_____	_____	How to visit for the Church
71.	_____	_____	_____	Basic Skills in Speechmaking
72.	_____	_____	_____	Creative Leisure
73.	_____	_____	_____	Customs in New Testament Times
74.	_____	_____	_____	Bearing Christian Influence in Daily Work
75.	_____	_____	_____	Democratic Process in Action
76.	_____	_____	_____	Homes that Teach
77.	_____	_____	_____	Current Questions in Theology
78.	_____	_____	_____	Improving Skills in Witnessing
79.	_____	_____	_____	Worship Practices Through the Ages
80.	_____	_____	_____	How to Study a Book of the Bible
81.	_____	_____	_____	How Adults Learn
82.	_____	_____	_____	Persons in Crisis
83.	_____	_____	_____	Growing a Christian Personality
84.	_____	_____	_____	Sign Language for Deaf Ministry
85.	_____	_____	_____	Spanish for Language Missions
86.	_____	_____	_____	Teaching the Mentally Retarded at Church

87. Other Subjects of Your Choice

Below is listed the program offered during the second year of the revised program:

ADULT TRAINING PROGRAM

Choose what you plan to study for the entire year and keep in your Bible for future reference.

First Period—September 13–October 18
(Choose one)
1. Life and Letters of Paul
2. Growing a Christian Personality
3. Sounds of the Seventies: Missions in Texas
4. Baptist History
5. Spanish for Language Missions
6. Sign Language for Deaf Ministry
7. New Member Orientation
8. Married Young People—The Spirit Filled Life
9. Student Career—Baptist Beliefs
10. Single Adult Department (30 years-up)
11. Senior Adult Department (60 years-up)

Second Period—October 25–November 29
(Choose one)
1. Archaeology and the Bible
2. Understanding Adults
3. Baptist Work in Fort Worth
4. Understanding Youth
5. Christians Confronting Communism
6. Spanish For Language Missions
7. Sign Language for Deaf Ministry
8. New Member Orientation
9. Married Young People—Christians Confronting Communism
10. Student Career—Ministering to Drug Abusers
11. Single Adult Department (30 years-up)
12. Senior Adult Department (60 years-up)

Third Period—Dec. 6–27
Mission Interpretation Programs: Foreign, Home, State, and Local Missions will be presented by missionaries on furlough and others who

have had first hand experience in these areas of mission work. (Details to be announced)

Fourth Period—January 3–February 7
(Choose one)

1. How to Interpret the Bible
2. Developing your Leadership Ability
3. Baptist Work with Drug Abusers and Alcoholics
4. Increasing your Personal Efficiency
5. Spanish for Language Missions
6. Sign Language for Deaf Ministry
7. New Member Orientation
8. Married Young People—Building a Successful Marriage
9. Student Career—Building a Successful Marriage

10, 11, Same as under Period One.

Fifth Period—February 14–March 21
(Choose one)

1. Revelation
2. How to Visit for the Church
3. Baptist Work in Juvenile Rehabilitation
4. Constructive Parent Child Relationships
5. Spanish for Language Missions
6. Sign Language for Deaf Ministry
7. New Member Orientation
8. Married Young People—Christian Family Money Management
9. Student Career—Increasing your Personal Efficiency

10, 11, Same as under Period One.

Special Home Missions Program—March 28

Sixth Period—April 4–May 9
(Choose One)

1. Old Testament Survey
2. Christian Life and Contemporary Times
3. Christianity and World Religions
4. Baptist Beliefs
5. Spanish for Language Missions
6. Sign Language for Deaf Ministry
7. New Member Orientation

8. Married Young People—Preparing for Parenthood
   9. Student Career—How to Interpret the Bible
   10, 11, Same as under Period One.

Girls' Training Organization (G.A.s)
Coronation—May 16

Seventh Period—May 23–June 27
(Choose one)
   1. New Testament Survey
   2. Bearing Christian Influences in Daily Work
   3. Baptist Work in Africa
   4. Building a Successful Marriage
   5. Spanish for Language Missions
   6. Sign Language for Deaf Ministry
   7. New Member Orientation
   8. Married Young People—Bible Interpretation
   9. Student Career—Archaeology and the Bible
   10, 11, Same as under Period One.

July 4—Special Patriotic Feature

Eighth Period—July 11–August 22
(Choose one)
   1. Counseling and Ministering to Individual Needs
   2. Christian View of Science and the Scriptures
   3. Baptist Work in the Orient
   4. Christian Responsibility to the Mass Media
   5. Spanish for Language Missions
   6. Sign Language for Deaf Ministry
   7. New Member Orientation
   8. Married Young People—Revelation
   9. Student Career—Revelation
   10, 11, Same as under Period One.

Boys' Training Organization (R.A.s)

Recognition Service—August 29

As was mentioned earlier, a promotion sheet is prepared and distributed in Adult Departments on Sunday morning. A typical example is shown below:

The Whole Family Learning for Action
SUNDAYS 5:45 P.M.
CHOOSE ONE for the Next 6 Weeks (April 4–May 9)

I. *OLD TESTAMENT SURVEY* (B125)
Teacher, Dr. Myrtle Wood
April 4 The Land and the Book
April 11 From Noah to Abraham
April 18 From Abraham to David
April 25 The Northern Kingdom to the Fall of Israel to the Assyrians
May 2 The Southern Kingdom to the Fall of Judah to Babylon
May 9 The Exile and Return

II. *BAPTISTS BELIEFS* (B124)
Teachers: Rev. Charles Redmond, James Hardin, Dr. Larry Walker, Rev. Tom Harris
April 4 The Bible
April 11 God and Man
April 18 Church
April 25 Salvation
May 2 Life After Death
May 8 Current Issues

III. *FORCES THAT MOLD US* (B122)
Teachers: L. E. Willcoxon, Ed York, Mrs. Ernest Byers
April 4 Molded by our Milieu
April 11 Formed by Friends, Fashions and Fads
April 18 Shaped by the School
April 25 Moved by the Movies
May 2 Prompted by the Printed
May 9 Affected by the Airways

IV. *CHRISTIANITY AND WORLD RELIGIONS* (B123)
April 4 Katherine Cozzens (Brazil)
April 11 South America
April 18 Ben Tomlinson (Taiwan)

April 25 Nobu Nakamoto (Japan)
May 2 Sid Schmidt (Malaysia)
May 9 Sid Schmidt (Malaysia)
V. *NEW MEMBER ORIENTATION* (A203)
Director: Charles Layton
VI. *SENIOR ADULTS* (B112)
Director: Bill Goodell
VII. *MARRIED YOUNG PEOPLE* (A107)
Teacher: Mrs. Dick Eudaly
"Green Letters"—Christian Growth and Development
VIII. *SINGLE BUSINESS & PROFESSIONAL* (A102)
Director: Mrs. Jenny Myra Stewart
IX. *SPANISH FOR LANGUAGE MISSIONS* (B110)
Teacher: Dick Eudaly
X. *SIGN LANGUAGE FOR DEAF MINISTRY* (A204)
Teacher: Mrs. Delmar Gentry
XI. *LITERACY: "IMPROVING YOUR READING* (B119)
Teacher: Rev. Henry Malone

YOUTH

I. *STUDENT CAREER* (A117)
Director: Tim Hedquist
II. *YOUTH-IN-ACTION* (Lower Sanctuary)
Bob Walters—Witnessing, One to One
III. *GRADE 7–9* (*Boys*)
Overcoming Doubts
Emotional Stability in Missions
IV. *GRADE 6* (*Girls*)
Why Should I?
People on the Move from Aware
V. *GRADE 5* (*Girls*)
Training Program
VI. *GRADE 4* (*Girls*)
Missions
VII. *GRADE 1–6* (*Boys*)
Concern for the Sick
Concern for the Lonely

VIII. *GRADE 2–3* (*Girls*)
　　What do Missionaries do
　　Learning about Jesus
 IX. *GRADE 1* (*Girls*)
　　Learning about Jesus
　　God Planned for Families

An Evaluation of the Adult Program

Looking back upon two full years of planning for the adult training program, it is obvious that some refinements are needed. First, we are convinced that efforts must be made to emphasize young adult units by age groups. This will enable a stronger fellowship element to be established. The questionnaire will continue to be used with this age group and with the entire adult division. However, in the young adult age range they may choose as a group all of their courses of study for the entire year. This will be done in the early fall as other adult courses are chosen. Secondly, a greater emphasis will be given to a more structured approach to leadership training. Persons will be enlisted to attend specific courses which will be taught in sequence throughout the year. As an example, Old Testament survey will be taught during the first period of study next year. During the second training period New Testament survey will be taught followed during the third period with Baptist history or Baptist beliefs. Also, running simultaneously with each of these will be such practical leadership courses, as developing your leadership ability, learning to work with groups, how to prepare a Sunday School lesson plan, the teacher as a counselor, and how to interpret the Bible.

Persons will be enlisted throughout the year to enter any one of these courses he has not previously taken. Sunday School department directors will be encouraged to enlist all workers to enter certain courses as a group.

Thirdly, more attention will be given to the use of reading assignments and home preparation. Teachers and leaders will suggest a course reading assignment during the first session of study. Along with this greater emphasis will be given to the use of audio-visuals and other teaching aids. Most teachers already do an excellent job at this point. Our audio-visual staff and the church library staff make needed items available.

A fourth consideration will be to offer more courses for the senior adult age range. These will be practical courses, such as Living on Limited Income During Retirement, (Social Security, Medicare, Pensions, Savings, etc.) Adjusting to Retirement, The Senior Adult and His Ministry in Retirement, The Senior Adult and Mission Action, and Using Leisure Time Wisely in Retirement. All of these will be designed to meet the personal needs of the age group and to provide outlets for service and usefulness after retirement.

Organization

A question is often asked, "What organization do you have for your adult training program?" It is our plan to have a convener for each course to oversee everything that takes place. It is his job to assist in enlisting teachers and leaders for his particular course, to provide equipment and materials needed, to see that each person attending is enrolled and has his attendance recorded each Sunday night. It is also his responsibility to return the records to the general secretary each week. On the beginning night of each training period all conveners help direct persons to the rooms where courses will be held.

The adult training director gives general direction for all courses of study other than the new member orientation program. It is his job to see that each course is well planned and that teachers are enlisted. He works with the missions training group just as he does with the other conveners to see that their course is well planned. When conveners have turned in their completed outlines of their course, the adult training director compiles them into a promotion sheet to be used on Sunday morning during adult department periods. As has been mentioned earlier, it is also used on the back of the Sunday bulletin for promotion purposes. The adult training director is also responsible for assigning rooms for each study, for putting up posters to give directions, and for working out any problem arising in the adult training program. He prepares the questionnaire, outlines the annual program of study, secures materials, and helps enlist teachers and leaders. Of course all of this is done in consultation with the general church training director, the minister of education, and the pastor. When courses are offered for age group workers, it is planned in consultation with the related staff member or age group coordinator. No personnel are invited from outside the congregation unless this is approved by the pastor.

Let us now turn our attention to other age groups.

Youth-in-Action

A unique program is provided for tenth, eleventh, and twelfth grade age groups. During our study it was recognized that this one group needed special consideration. In the church study committee recommendations it was suggested that activities be planned to provide special programs "aimed toward youth outreach and characterized by testimonies, special speakers, musical groups, drama, and informational programs." The key idea involved in this concept was that quality programs would be provided. It was hoped that many of these programs would be of such great interest that our own young people would be anxious to invite their classmates, friends, and acquaintances from school and from their own neighborhoods. From time to time outstanding personalities have been brought in for the purpose of giving our own young people a "talking point" to be used in interesting their age group to attend.

Generally these young people meet as one large group. Four committees are set up to provide one program each month. Young adult couples are enlisted to serve with each committee as counselors. In late summer themes are selected for each month of the coming year and programs are generally built around these themes. Occasionally, however, special events are planned which do not necessarily relate to the pre-selected theme. Examples of some program themes are:

Youth-in-Action Schedule

Jan. 25 Phil Driscoll trumpeter and speaker from Baylor

Feb. 1 Dialogue and feedback session on Youth-In-Action

        8   The Spurrlows
       15   Flipside, a movie to answer the questions of young people in America about morals today.
       22   Steve and Mike Stroup, young men from Dallas who started a morning prayer group in their high school that has grown from 6 to 450 in a year.

Mar.   1   The Immortals, a folksinging group from White Settlement Baptist church.
        8   Dick Greenwood, missionary journeyman, on his experiences
       22   Jeff Woolwine, Travis member and Evangelist

Apr.   5   Jo Ann Shelton
       19   Mel Brown, on Pastoral care in Hospitals and Jail
       26   O.B.U. Singing group

May   3   Marge Caldwell
       10   Moody Science Film
       17   Drama by our own young people.

From time to time music groups or special personalities are invited in from outside the congregation. They are normally selected to appeal not only to our own youth, but to young people outside of "Christian circles." Parts of these programs may be secular in nature but always a recognition is made of the fact that the group is gathered because of a common faith that our youth have in Jesus Christ. No groups are invited in unless they are able to share a testimony of a growing Christian faith.

Youth-in-Action meets from 5:15 to 6:45 P.M. each Sunday. The first forty-five minutes are used for a youth choir rehearsal while the last forty-five minutes are used for the program. This choir rehearsal has proven to be a stabilizing and reenforcing element to this youth group. Of course there are some young people who do not participate in the music program. They are usually involved in providing staging, technical assistance, or dramatic scenes for musical productions presented by the choir. Some who choose not to participate in the choir come at six o'clock for the program.

One Sunday out of each month is set aside for visitation. Young people meet at the church at 4:30 P.M. and go out to visit for one hour. They invite prospects to attend the program to be provided on that same night. Prospects are assigned on Sunday morning through Sunday School departments. Some young people visit friends and acquaintances from their school. This visitation and the musical productions help give the element of action to this program.

During special seasons of the year a Sunday night may be given over to visiting shut-ins or to carrying out other activities of a missions-action nature.

Though this group meets normally as one large group for their programs, there are times when smaller groups are used for discussion and fellowship. This is determined by the content of the program. It is recognized that there is great value in small group activities, especially as they give an element of organized structure to the overall program.

The content of the program takes in the entire spectrum of Christian knowledge, faith, and works. Programs grow out of the interest and needs of this age group and deal with ethical issues as well as missions, doctrine, history, and other subjects studied in the Training Union curriculum.

Preschool, Children, and Junior High Training

Our missions education program and our church training program for these age groups were also combined into a single program and meets on Sunday night during the church training hour. Leaders are responsible to the church for providing a curriculum which includes units of study from missions materials and church training materials.

This was initially begun by asking the missions organizations of Girls Auxiliary, Royal Ambassadors, and Sunbeams to change their meeting time from Wednesday night to Sunday night. All age groups, first grade through ninth grade are separated by sex. The girls are called G.T.O., Girls Training Organization, and the boys are called B.T.O., Boys Training Organization.

It is understood that both groups will be fully able to accomplish the steps or ranks of advancement promoted by the missions agencies for Girl's Auxiliary and Royal Ambassadors. However, it is also understood that each of these groups will select units of study from curriculum materials provided by both the Sunday School Board and the missions agencies.

The setting up of the curriculum is done at a planning meeting before promotion time each fall. At this meeting all units of study are selected for the entire church year. Leaders secure a complete list of units of study which are to be published by the missions agencies and by the Church Training Department for the coming year. Units are chosen from both sets of materials. The intent is that we will have a complete and balanced program of training for our boys and girls and that the steps of recognition promoted by the missions agencies will be included in the program.

Separate recognition programs are scheduled for the boys and for the girls. Both are held during the church training hour with all age groups attending. The girls have their service in May and the boys have theirs in August.

Training Records

Every effort has been made to keep the records for the church training program as simple as possible. Our record forms are outlined below.

In the adult divisions an individual record card is used. It serves as an enrollment as well as attendance record.

On the first night a person attends a training course he is asked to fill in the above card and to check himself present for that session. These cards are collected by the course convener and are formed into a study group record book. The cover card serves also as a summary record card for the study group.

On the second Sunday night of the course the convener checks

143 Training with a Purpose

ATTENDANCE RECORD
for Adult Studies

Session( )   Special Participation

1_____

2_____

3_____

4_____

5_____

6_____

7_____

NAME _____ PHONE _____

ADDRESS _____ ZIP CODE _____

SUNDAY SCHOOL DEPARTMENT _____

TITLE OF COURSE _____ DATE _____

CHURCH TRAINING REPORT

for Adult Groups

Date	Enrolled	Present

TITLE of COURSE _____

CONVENER _____ ROOM NO _____

NEW CHURCH MEMBER ATTENDANCE RECORD									
COUNSELING || INSTRUCTION								
C-1	C-2	1	2	3	4	5	6	7	SUMMARY SESSION
Meaning of Conversion	Meaning of Church Member	New Life & Growth As A Christian	Your Bible & Its Use	Your Church & Its Covenant	Your Church & Its Beliefs	Church Working Together & With Others	Church & Its History	Your Church & Your Home --- Sharing Your Faith	
date	date	date	date	date	date	date	date	date	date

NAME_____ ADDRESS_____
(Last name first)

BIRTHDATE_____ PHONE NUMBER_____

DATE ENROLLED_____ COUNSELOR_____

TEACHER_____ Adult   Y.P.   Int.   Jr.   Pri.
(circle age group)

each person present either by having him fill in an individual record slip or by observing who is present and marking the record book.

When the course is concluded, individual record cards are filed in the office along with study course awards. This becomes a permanent record of training for each person who attends.

In new member orientation a different record form is used for all age groups.

When persons complete New Member Orientation this card is also placed in his training file and kept in the church office.

All other age groups, youth, children, and preschool, have a simple form which is used to record attendance only. Workers have the same card and are checked only on attendance. In larger groups of the youth division individuals are asked to write their names on small slips of paper which are used by a secretary to check their attendance records. The record card used by the youth, children and preschool divisions is shown on page 145.

ATTENDANCE RECORD

Sunday School (Pre-School — 3rd Grade)
Training Program (Pre-School — Youth)

	1st Sunday	2nd Sunday	3rd Sunday	4th Sunday	5th Sunday
OCTOBER					
NOVEMBER					
DECEMBER					
JANUARY					
FEBRUARY					
MARCH					

	1st Sunday	2nd Sunday	3rd Sunday	4th Sunday	5th Sunday
APRIL					
MAY					
JUNE					
JULY					
AUGUST					
SEPTEMBER					

BIRTHDAY _____ PHONE _____   Additional information

NAME _____

ADDRESS _____

CHURCH MEMBER _____ CHURCH? _____

Father: _____ CHURCH? _____

Mother: _____ CHURCH? _____

CONCLUSION

Thus we have sought to tell the Travis Avenue story. It is one which has produced an exciting era for our church. However, we are thoroughly convinced that the story has just begun. This book merely serves as an introduction to what we firmly believe God plans to do through our church.

Each day we become more convinced that "people can be reached *now*." May some of these methods be helpful to this end. Above all may the basic philosophy of "outreach" serve as a challenge and inspiration to churches everywhere to put "first things first" and reach people *NOW* for Christ!

APPENDIX
OTHER IDEAS AND SUGGESTIONS

Bus Outreach Program

There are many pitfalls to avoid in establishing a bus program. Some of these pitfalls are given in the following paragraphs and are not considered to be a complete list.

1. Don't expect buying or renting buses will automatically insure that you will reach great numbers of people. In one bus conference a pastor related the story of how his church purchased five buses, set up a schedule of bus stops, passed out handbills throughout the community and then went out on the first Sunday to pick up riders. No one rode on that first day. Within a few weeks the pastor, as well as the members of the church, had decided that the whole idea just would not work for their church. This pastor went on to point out that his church was now wanting to sell the buses and asked if there were those present who would be interested in buying them.

It goes without saying that the bus outreach program requires a great deal of preparation, continuous visitation, and just plain hard work to make it go.

2. Don't expect all members to be in favor of the bus outreach program. Certainly no matter what program we undertake there will be some who will not respond to it, and yet church leaders have every responsibility to see that they lead out in such a way that members will want to see a given program succeed.

Two suggestions are offered here: involve the people in a study and a decision to begin the bus outreach program and then call on a broad cross section of the people to help enlist riders for the new buses. As was pointed out in the chapter on busing, the Sunday School at Travis Avenue led the church in canvassing 400 blocks to begin our first four buses. This means that approximately 400 individuals became personally involved in getting this program under way.

3. Don't expect the bus outreach program to pay for itself. Every church must understand that the bus outreach program will primarily reach older preschoolers on up through the sixth- and seventh-grade age groups. There will be some adults and a few older youth, but the experience of most churches is that children are reached through this program.

It is quite possible, however, that creative ways will be discovered in the days ahead for reaching more adults. Perhaps more adults have been reached through the buses than are evident. Experience has shown that when the father begins to ride the bus, very often the family rides in their own automobile and no longer on the bus. At Travis, however, the bus outreach program has brought excitement to our people and many have increased their contributions.

We are also convinced that many young adults have been attracted to our church because of the mission nature of the bus outreach program. Not only have we had to expand our Sunday School departments in the areas of the children reached through the bus ministry, but we have also added new departments for toddlers who have come as their parents have been attracted to the church.

4. Don't feel that your church must conduct a bus outreach program just like another church. Some communities are different; some churches are different. Some churches will buy their buses, others will rent theirs. The important thing is that we consider the use of this approach and then determine the most effective way that it can be carried out in our local situation.

5. Don't sink too much money into expensive buses. Most buses will operate within a few miles of the church. Seldom will a bus need to go outside the city limits. This means that used buses can often serve the purpose for a local church. Churches wishing to have a bus to make long trips for choir tours or to Glorieta or Ridgecrest certainly may want to consider a new bus with the capability for distant travel. Used buses can often be purchased at prices ranging from as low as $400 up to $2,000. New buses range in price from $6,000 to $10,000 or $12,000 if they are the school bus type. Some buses cost as much as $30,000 to $40,000. A church simply must consider the purpose in using the bus and then decide what would be best to buy.

6. Avoid the pitfall of building the bus outreach program on the children. A study of one budget showed that a church spent an average of fifteen cents per child per week in providing kites, toys, or other such items. It has not been necessary to provide this kind of motivation at Travis Avenue and in many other churches. It is our feeling that money that is available for the purpose of promotion of the bus outreach program can be better spent by providing activities for the boys and girls. These activities might include special field trips to the zoo, to a park for a picnic, or to other places which would add to the enrichment of these young lives.

7. Don't assume that your church must set up a separate organization for bus outreach. The Sunday School is the organization to do this job. Many churches make the mistake of providing a different organization or different committee to handle every program imagi-

nable. It is recommended here that a Sunday School officer called the bus outreach director be set up to lead out in this program. Bus captains are considered to be on a par of the department directors at Travis Avenue and from time to time are invited to meet with the department directors for planning. Unwholesome attitudes have developed in some churches between the Sunday School and the bus workers. Much of this kind of problems can be avoided by helping them understand their close relationship as an outreach team.

8. Don't allow the bus outreach program to become a child evangelism program. Some churches who use bus outreach programs have been accused of baptizing children three and four years of age and have actually used child evangelism materials. This raises the whole question of baptized believers. Certainly we want to be concerned in presenting the gospel to every child or adult so that he can make his personal commitment to Christ.

9. Don't steal riders. Another criticism that has come to some churches is that of taking riders from other churches. The leaders of the bus outreach program must set the pattern here and keep before the workers that this is not appropriate. The question that can be asked to avoid this kind of problem is, "Do you attend another church?" It has been our policy to reach out for any person who does not actually attend another church. Our workers are instructed that if a person does attend another church, they are to encourage him to attend his own church on the very next Sunday. This kind of spirit can help us honor God and build Christian fellowship among other churches.

10. Avoid lengthy visits on Saturday. The purpose of the Saturday visitation should be primarily to visit regular riders and to enlist new riders. Our workers are encouraged to visit briefly at the door in order to seek a commitment for each family member to ride on Sunday morning. One half of the time is to be spent canvassing new areas to enlist new riders.

Although bus workers are encouraged to witness to parents, youth, and children, concerning their relationship to Christ, they are discouraged from doing this kind of work on Saturday. Experience has shown that the first priority on Saturday must be enlisting the riders to come for Sunday. Experience has also shown that more people will be won through bus outreach if the bus workers enlist the riders and briing them into Sunday School and worship services where they can be presented the gospel message. Workers, however, are encouraged to visit during the week or after they have done their Saturday enlistment visitation.

11. Avoid the halfhearted worker. The bus outreach program, as perhaps few other programs throughout the church, must have workers who are willing to give a definite visitation effort every single week if the program is to move forward. The halfhearted worker can be expensive when you consider the cost of buses and the necessity for visitation every week.

12. Don't entrust a bus route to a Sunday School class, a mission group, or a youth group. Generally it has proven to be best to enlist a definite worker who will be responsible for each bus route week after week. If other groups are used, it should be understood that one person is to carry the responsibility and will be responsible to the bus outreach director for the route.

13. Don't allow workers on the team who do not understand their duties. It should be understood that the captain is in charge of the route and that workers must attend the Saturday bus meeting or whatever planning meeting is held. Also the bus worker needs to know that he is expected to be present on Sunday except when on vacation or ill. Workers who do not know their responsibilities can certainly keep a route from making the progress that it should.

14. Don't assume that all workers are good visitors. Some persons do apparently have more natural ability for visitation than others. Yet all workers can improve their ability to visit through training. Have good visitors demonstrate how to make an effective visit.

15. Don't feel that a good beginning in your bus outreach pro-

gram will insure continued success. This program requires an every week effort. Critical times, such as the Christmas holidays and others must be carefully worked out. Perhaps a limited schedule can be considered for holiday periods, but some effort should be made every week to keep the routes progressing. New workers will have to be enlisted as time goes on. Some workers may be unable to continue working for various personal reasons. Some have work schedules that change. Also new workers are needed in order to expand the bus outreach program. Improved methods are required, especially as the program expands. It is important that those who lead in this work continually keep the significance of the work before the church and the workers.

16. Don't allow bus workers to become an elite group of "holier than thou" persons. It has been interesting to note that this question is often brought up in bus conferences. It seems to go back to the idea of whether the bus workers are considered to be a part of the team in the Sunday School or whether they are developed as a separate group apart from other workers in the church. This has not become a problem in our church apparently because the Sunday School from the very beginning was involved in canvassing to enlist riders. But workers have also been involved in various plans for outreach through the Sunday School. Church leaders should be careful to see that the bus captains and workers as well as the Sunday School workers and other leaders share alike when recognitions are given.

17. Don't overlook safety. Although it is not necessary to have all new buses, it is necessary to have a bus that is road-safe. Safety inspections in keeping with the state standard for school buses is a good guide for churches to use in insuring the safety of their buses. Adequate insurance, of course, is essential. Good drivers are a necessity. Some churches have found it necessary to limit driving to persons who pass a certain test. Every effort should be made to insure that the question of safety is properly considered.

18. Don't assume that the whole family will be reached by the bus workers alone. It seems that if the entire family is to be reached,

Sunday School workers in every age group must be assigned to visit all family members to cultivate them. Teen-agers need to be assigned to teen-age departments; parents to adult departments, etc.

19. Don't expand bus outreach unless adequate space and teachers can be provided. It is certainly a mistake to go to the trouble and expense of reaching great numbers on our buses unless we are able to see that a quality program of teaching and training and worship can be provided for those who come. Care should be taken to keep enrolment ceilings in line if good teaching is to take place. Workers need to be enlisted and trained in order that a proper pupil-teacher ratio can be maintained. Perhaps no group of boys and girls in all of our Sunday School need individual attention so much as many of the boys and girls who come on our buses.

20. Don't let the size of your church keep you out of a bus outreach program. Some churches feel that they are too small to enter into bus outreach. Perhaps there are instances where it would be inadvisable to start such a program but almost every church in every community could use one bus and could reach a number of boys and girls and some adults. The bus itself could be used for a classroom in order to provide needed space for adults or youth.

21. Don't expect the bus captain and visitors to be Sunday School workers. It is especially difficult for the bus captain to do the necessary visitation throughout the week and on Saturday, to bring the boys and girls on Sunday, get them into their classrooms, and at the same time be expected to teach a Sunday School class. The time and energy required to prepare a lesson and to visit for the class need to be spent in building the bus route. There may be times when this will be necessary, but it seems wise to have bus captains and workers freed from other Sunday School responsibilities.

Making "Time Change Day" Count

For two years after daylight saving time was instigated in our state, we noted that on the last Sunday of April, when the time changed from central standard time to daylight saving time, our Sunday School attendance dropped by two to three hundred. This was likely because people had not made the adjustment necessary to get up an hour earlier to get to Sunday School. It seems that our churches take the brunt of the time change so that business and industry can have the benefit of the weekend for people to get used to the change.

Our response to this past year proved to be helpful. On the last Sunday in April we saw our attendance increase by almost 900 over the previous year. We simply stayed on the old time and worked for a high attendance. A great effort was made to promote the idea of "don't touch the clock; don't change the time." It was explained that we would have a "time change ceremony" at the close of the morning worship service. At that time the pastor asked everyone to change his watch from 12:00 noon to 1:00 P.M.

It was anticipated that some would become confused and would come early, so coffee and doughnuts were provided. Only eleven persons actually came early out of the 2,348 who attended on this day. Most of these had not been contacted by their classes, had not read the church paper, had been out of the city, or simply had not received word of the plan.

The overall result of this approach was that our people were surprised and pleased to see our all-time high attendance record broken. Our people did not have to get up early to get to Sunday School. They simply waited until noon to change to daylight saving time. We experienced victory rather than defeat. A potentially bad day was turned into a fruitful day. Attendance jumped from 1,466 the previous year to 2,348. This was an increase of 882 or 60 percent. No doubt this will be an annual event each spring. *Good promotion is absolutely essential or people will become greatly confused.*

Vacation Bible School on Saturday and Sunday

There were three primary reasons for having Vacation Bible School on Saturday and Sunday—cost, extra teaching time, and outreach follow-up. By having Vacation Bible School on Saturday and

Sunday we had many unchurched boys and girls for seven days in one week and ran our buses only seven times, including Parent's Day, rather than nine times, including Parents' Night, for an eight-day school. Since the buses already ran on Sunday, only six extra bus runs were required—a saving of $1,260 (15 buses at $28 each per day). Also by having Parents' Day on Sunday we were able to get the entire family into our regular Sunday morning program. Many barriers were broken down through this.

As has been indicated, Sunday was designated as Parents' Day. This was carried out as follows: The weekday schedule for Vacation Bible School was set up to coincide with our Sunday morning schedule. It began on all seven days at 9:30 A.M. and concluded at noon.

2. It was emphasized from the very beginning that Vacation Bible School would continue through Saturday and Sunday.

3. A special class was set up for parents of children who came to Vacation Bible School but were not normally in our Sunday School—seventy-eight parents attended. A special Bible-centered program was worked related to parent and children in the home and Vacation Bible School activities, and our regular Sunday School and worship program.

4. Vacation Bible School workers continued to use the same rooms and to lead out on Sunday morning just as they had all through the week.

5. Sunday School workers who were not working in Vacation Bible School were asked to be present in their regular departments in order to become acquainted with new boys and girls reached through Vacation Bible School. Our hope was that these could be reached by the Sunday School workers for Sunday School each week.

6. Adult teachers who worked in Vacation Bible School were asked to secure a substitute teacher to take their places in their regular Sunday School departments.

7. Youth departments combined their classes, since literally scores of teen-agers were working in the Vacation Bible School departments.

8. Refreshments were served to preschool children just as on other days with our senior adults doing the serving. Preschoolers did not participate in the morning worship service outlined below.

9. Our schedule was altered as follows for Vacation Bible School Parents' Day.

	Normal	Parents' Day
Sunday School	9:30–10:40	9:30–10:30
Worship	11:00–12:00	10:45–11:45
Open House	none	11:45–12:25

10. The worship service was aimed toward the Parents' Day theme. School-age boys and girls marched in and were seated by departments. Visiting parents were seated in a special place. The service proceeded as a normal Sunday morning worship service with a brief report of Vacation Bible School at announcement time. The pastor preached an evangelistic message to parents, to the school, and to all present.

11. Open house followed the worship service with refreshments at key locations throughout the building. Boys and girls marched to their departments to wait for their parents to visit.

Results. No special emphasis was placed upon attendance and yet we experienced our highest summer attendance on record, 2,054. Our people were thrilled. A number of parents and boys and girls made their professions of faith. More than 1,800 were enrolled in this Vacation Bible School which averaged 1,430 (excluding Saturday and Sunday), and seventy professions of faith were recorded. This was a tremendous victory for our people. Many gave sacrificially of their time to make this possible. Only God knows the full results of this experience. Many new families were reached and numerous other homes have been opened for meaningful cultivation and follow-up.

September Promotion

This year we promoted in September for the first time departing from our regular first Sunday in October Promotion Day. The main reason for this was to get an early start into the fall program. Families seemed to be ready and willing to settle down from summer vacations into a new school year. We also wanted to spread the fall calendar of activities over this additional month. Activities in the fall are often crowded and this extra month hopefully will allow for better spacing of events. We also felt that we could build attendance in September more easily if promotion were at the start of the month.

How was this done? This idea has been discussed among our workers over the last year or two and finally was recommended to the church by the Sunday School department directors. We decided not to worry about the problem of the Labor Day holiday but to go on and promote on that day anyway. The biggest problem to be faced was that of lesson materials for our Preschool, Children's, and Youth Divisions. Age-group workers went to work on this problem and worked it out as follows:

Preschool, Children's, and Youth teachers' quarterlies were promoted along with the pupils to the new teachers. This was to some extent cumbersome and some adaptions had to be worked out. Actually all pupils continued on their same units of study throughout the month of September, and then when October came, they began with the new quarterlies and the new year of study. This proved to be less of a problem than was anticipated.

The results of September promotion have proven to be good thus far. The Sunday School year has been kicked off a month earlier and certainly it has helped to spread out the fall program. September average attendance has been remarkable and has increased as follows:

1968	1,568
1969	1,603
1970	1,715
1971	2,147

Labor Day proved to be a good day although certainly it was not the banner day that promotion usually is. Last year, 1,625 were present while 1,968 were present this year.

The only aspect of September promotion that seems to have been a problem was that of enlistment of workers during the month of

August. Many people are still on vacation during this month and are not available for enlistment. We feel, however, that the experience workers had this year will prove to make enlistment easier next year. All in all we were extremely well pleased and plan to continue September promotion in the days ahead.

Baptist Women

Since the church originally approved the recommendations concerning Woman's Missionary Union general meetings (p. 26), one change has been made. Missions action groups now have a quarterly general meeting.

The idea of eliminating the general meeting as can be noted in the recommendation mentioned above, grew out of the fact that a missions study would be offered on every Sunday night. The hope was to involve both men and women in missions education more often so that a wider range of studies could be undertaken. Also, the entire month of December is given over entirely to missions education and a special home missions emphasis is presented on a churchwide basis in the spring with Woman's Missionary Union leaders in charge.

The quarterly meetings which have now been initiated will allow for additional mission studies and other special emphases aimed toward the ladies who do not work out of their homes. The Sunday night studies are particularly attractive to those who do work out of their homes. Our ladies are free to set up meetings as often as they are deemed wise as long as they are scheduled during weeks other than our "Special Outreach Weeks."

Our church is committed to the cause of missions education and mission action and is anxious to explore every avenue for bringing it about. We are confident that our people are becoming more missions conscious week by week. Almost every week now we are hearing reports of mission action projects Sunday School classes have carried out, whereas in the past this was not so.